# Adopting
# a child
## The definitive guide to
## adoption in the UK

Jenifer Lord

Published by
British Association for Adoption & Fostering
(BAAF)
Saffron House
6–10 Kirby Street
London EC1N 8TS
www.baaf.org.uk

Charity registration 275689 (England and Wales),
SC039337 (Scotland)

© BAAF, 1984, 1986, 1990, 1995, 1998, 2002,
2005, 2006, 2008, 2011, 2013

British Library Cataloguing in Publication Data
A catalogue record for this book is available from
the British Library

ISBN 978 1 910039 01 4

Cover design: mecob.org
Cover photograph: © Siri Stafford/Getty Images
All photographs posed by models
Designed by Helen Joubert Designs
Typeset by Fravashi Aga
Printed in Great Britain by T J International

BAAF is the leading UK-wide membership
organisation for all those concerned with
adoption, fostering and child care issues.

# Contents

## Acknowledgements

The first four editions of *Adopting A Child* were co-authored by Prue Chennells and Chris Hammond in 1984, 1986, 1990 and 1995. Jenifer Lord made considerable revisions for the fifth edition in 1998, and in subsequent editions. This edition draws on the previous editions but contains new material and amendments in light of recent government initiatives and of legislative changes in the UK.

The author would like to thank John Simmonds, BAAF, for helpful information on current practice; Katrina Wilson, BAAF, and Andy Stott, Adoption Register for England and Wales, for their efficient help with statistical information; Catherine Mullin, BAAF Northern Ireland, for helpful information in relation to Northern Ireland; and Jo Francis, Publications Department, BAAF, for her work in producing this edition.

The quotations in this book have been taken from several sources:
Personal communication to the author
*Adopted Children Speaking*, BAAF, 1999
*Looking after our Own*, BAAF, 2005
*Could you be my Parent?*, BAAF, 2005
*Adoption Today*, Adoption UK
*Foster Care* magazine, Fostering Network
*Be My Parent*
*From China with Love*, Wiley, 2006
*Frozen*, BAAF, 2010
*The Pink Guide to Adoption*, BAAF, 2009
*The Family Business*, BAAF, 2008
*The Colours in Me*, BAAF, 2009
*Adoption Undone*, BAAF, 2007
*Special Guardianship in Practice*, BAAF, 2010
*Recipes for Fostering*, BAAF, 2009
*Gay, Lesbian and Heterosexual Adoptive Families,* BAAF, 2013
*Finding our Familia,* BAAF, 2012
*Related by Adoption,* BAAF, 2012

## The author

Jenifer Lord was for many years a child placement consultant who worked in BAAF's Southern England office. She is also the author of *The Adoption Process in England*, and has co-authored *Effective Adoption Panels, Effective Fostering Panels* and *Together or Apart? Assessing siblings for permanent placement.*

# Introduction

Around 5,670 children are currently adopted each year in the UK.*
Well over three-quarters, around 4,640, of these are children who
have been looked after by a local authority. The others are
predominantly children adopted by their parent and step-parent, and
about 150 are children who have been brought from overseas and
adopted by people living in the UK. There is a chapter in this book
addressed to step-families considering adoption and one to people
considering adopting from overseas. The rest of this book is about the
adoption of children who are looked after by local authorities. There
is also a chapter on meeting these children's needs through fostering.

There are currently nearly 93,000 children looked after by local
authorities in the UK, about two-thirds of them living in foster
homes. Many looked after children will return home to their family
within a year.

The number of looked after children who are adopted has risen
slightly in recent years. It represents a tiny proportion, about 5 per
cent, of all looked after children. Over 70 per cent of the looked
after children adopted recently in England were aged between one
and four. In Scotland, too, this pre-school age group of children
formed a significant percentage of children placed for adoption with
under-five-year-olds being the largest group. This reflects the wishes
of many adopters to parent pre-school children and the relative ease
with which adoption agencies are able to recruit adopters for young
children. It doesn't reflect the needs of many waiting children for
whom new families are urgently needed.

Children who wait for adoption tend to be older. There are single
children but many are in groups of brothers and sisters who need

* Figures are estimated, based on information available from different parts of the
UK. There are some variations in the detail of what is collected and the most
recent figures available but efforts have been made to ensure that the overall
picture is realistic.

placement together. There are children with disabilities who range in age from babies upwards. There are children from a huge variety of ethnic, religious and cultural backgrounds. Many of the children have been abused and/or neglected before they are taken into local authority care and they will have been further confused and upset by uncertainty and moves after coming into care.

Just as there is a wide range of children needing adoption, so will a wide range of people be welcomed by adoption agencies to adopt them. People of every ethnic, religious and cultural background, couples and single people – heterosexual as well as lesbian and gay, both with or without children – older people, people who have been divorced, all can and do become successful adoptive parents. And the great majority of adoptions work out well. Like all parents, adoptive parents get huge joy and satisfaction from parenting their children, as well as finding it very hard work and sometimes frustrating and painful.

Traditionally, adoption, for children not previously known to the families adopting them, was seen as severing connections with the past and starting afresh. Now it is understood how important it is to provide adoptive parents with as much information as possible to pass on to their children, and how important their heritage is for those children. Many adopted children continue to maintain important relationships – sometimes with their birth parents, more often with other family members like brothers and sisters, grandparents, aunts and uncles.

Adoption agencies do not expect you to know all about adoption before you approach them. They will provide information and opportunities for you to find out about what will be involved, for instance, by introducing you to experienced adoptive parents. They are also working hard to provide better help and support to you and your child once you are living together and after you have adopted. Help is also available from adoptive parents' support groups and, in England and Wales, from post-adoption centres.

We hope that this book will answer most of your initial questions as well as clarify anything that may have previously puzzled you about adoption – the processes, the cost, the legal issues, etc. All these and many other issues are addressed in this book. These are illustrated with real life experiences in which people candidly talk about what went right and what went wrong and how they were helped or helped themselves create a safe, secure and loving family environment for a child or children who needed this. For children who have to be separated from their birth families, having a new permanent family by adoption is an experience that must fulfil *their* needs and help them through to a fulfilling adulthood.

A glossary of terms that are used in this book and which may be unfamiliar to you is provided at the end.

## Adoption legislation

The Adoption and Children Act 2002 was fully implemented in England and Wales in December 2005. It is underpinned by more than ten sets of regulations and also by Statutory Guidance.

In Scotland, the Adoption and Children (Scotland) Act 2007 came into force in September 2009.

There are National Minimum Standards for adoption work in England and Wales and National Care Standards for adoption work in Scotland. These standards form the basis for inspection of adoption services.

Your local BAAF office or a local adoption agency will be able to give you up-to-date information and there are links to the Standards and legislation on www.baaf.org.uk.

Adoption is changing and developing and it will be important for you to check with BAAF and/or with a local adoption agency about any significant changes at the time you make your initial enquiries.

## Scope of this edition

The content of this edition applies to England, where some new
adoption regulations and statutory guidance were introduced in
2013. Much of it also applies to Wales and Scotland, and quite a
lot to Northern Ireland, although recognising that there are
variations between the different countries. *Adopting a Child in
Scotland* was published by BAAF in 2013 for prospective adopters
living in Scotland.

Adoption as a legal process was first established in 1926 in England
and Wales, in 1929 in Northern Ireland, and in 1930 in Scotland.
Although these are separate jurisdictions, the legal framework for
adoption was very similar and was primarily about legal security for
babies relinquished by their birth parents. Now that most children
placed for adoption with non-relatives have spent a period looked
after by the local authority, planning for them must also take
account of other child care legislation. There is wider variation in this
between Scotland and England and Wales, especially given the role
of the Children's Hearing system in Scotland. Devolution too is
playing more of a part. The statutory basis for the service is first of
all in the primary legislation and then in the regulations that provide
more detail.

There is one Adoption and Children Act for England and Wales but
separate regulations. Scotland will continue to have its own
legislation and regulations for all aspects of adoption. Northern
Ireland has tended to look towards that of England and Wales in
developing its legislation.

However, there are some differences in practice and procedures.
In Northern Ireland there are still a small number of babies who
come into or are removed to care at a very early age and proceed
to adoption. Adoption as a route out of care for older children in
Northern Ireland continues to be developed.

As stated previously, much of the text that follows will be relevant to
any part of the UK but more information about local variations can
be obtained from BAAF's regional centres (see Chapter 10). The

legislation provides for children moving from one legal jurisdiction to another so that children can be linked with families across the UK.

Just as the law has been updated over the 80-plus years that legal adoption has been possible, so practice has changed tremendously. The rest of this book will tell you more about this. One aspect of this that affects the delivery of adoption services is the change in local government. At first, much of the adoption service was provided by voluntary adoption agencies. Now there are fewer such agencies and most children placed are the responsibility of their local authority Social Services or Social Work Departments, which also act as adoption agencies to recruit and prepare adopters. A number of councils have been looking at different ways of delivering services. Social services may now be joined with education or housing services so that where reference is made to Social Services or Social Work Departments or Directors, you may need to check the precise names/designations locally. Although these terms are not accurate when applied to Northern Ireland, we have used them for the sake of simplicity. In Northern Ireland, personal social services are provided by five Health and Social Care Trusts.

A list of all agencies appears later on in this book.

# 01

# Children needing adoption

*Being adopted is great because you know who you are with a family who cares for you and loves you very much. I know it may be hard to leave your parents but you know they can't look after you, but they can write to you and they will always love you.*

Harriet, *The Colours in Me*

Possibly around 4,000 children currently in the care system in the UK could be placed for adoption with families if the families were available. Although the children are very different, they all have one thing in common: a need for a family.

It is recognised that, for nearly all children, life in a family is best. A new family can bring love and security to the child – and a child can bring joy and satisfaction to the family. Every child is different and brings the potential for different sorts of satisfaction just as they will bring their own set of needs and challenges. The agency's job, with your help, is to match that child's potential and needs with your abilities and expectations.

## Are there any babies needing adoption?

Of the 3,980 looked after children adopted in England in the year to March 2013, just 90 were babies under one. Proportionate figures for Scotland are similar. Today it is easier for women to choose to parent on their own and fewer single mothers are placing their babies for adoption. Contraception is more efficient than it used to be, and fewer unplanned pregnancies occur. It is also easier to terminate pregnancies than previously.

There are more white people interested in adopting a white baby without disabilities than there are such babies needing adoption. Agencies have little difficulty in finding suitable adopters for white babies without disabilities. This means that people who want to adopt only such a child are likely to find it hard even to get started on the adoption process and may not be able to adopt a baby.

However, agencies are somewhat less successful at finding black families or those from other minority ethnic groups, although they are getting better at it. This means that if you and/or your partner are black or from a minority ethnic group, you are more likely to find an agency to take up your application quite quickly. You will probably have a shorter wait before being linked with a baby, although this will vary as only quite small numbers of black babies and those from other minority ethnic groups are placed for adoption each year. If you can consider slightly older children, your wait could be shorter.

There are babies with disabilities or disabling conditions such as cerebral palsy and Foetal Alcohol Spectrum Disorder who need to be adopted. There are also some babies with genetic factors in their background, such as schizophrenia or Huntington's Chorea, for whom it is not always easy to find adoptive families.

## Toddlers and pre-school children

Children aged between one and five are the largest group of children adopted in the UK. This reflects the wishes of many adopters to parent pre-school children and the relative ease with which adoption agencies are able to recruit adopters for young children. The majority of these placements work out extremely successfully. However, these children often have complex needs. They may have been abused and neglected and given little opportunity to make attachments to reliable parent figures. They may be very confused about all that has happened in their short lives and unable to trust in anyone. In addition, there may also be uncertainties about their development which may not be resolved until they are older. Families need to be able to take on these issues and to access support and advice.

## What about older children?

Many children waiting to be adopted are aged five or over. They may have lived for some years with one or both of their parents, or other family members, or they may have had many moves in and out of foster homes, and the damage done by these experiences can last a very long time. Older children need especially resilient parents who can help them face up to the past – including their possible need to keep in touch with some members of their family – and see them through the difficult adolescent years to maturity. In a loving and secure home, most of these children will eventually begin to thrive, although the older they are, the longer it may take.

Children who have been looked after by a local authority for months or years are likely to have emotional and behavioural problems because of the experiences which led to them having to be separated from their birth families, but also because of not having a permanent parent figure in their lives. Even young children soon learn that there isn't much point in getting attached to an adult who is soon going to disappear out of their lives. They may find it difficult to become attached to a new family and are likely to test out their new parents with challenging behaviour. Young children may be more like babies in their behaviour sometimes, and even teenagers may act like very young children. But most children of all ages can eventually settle when they realise that they really are part of the family.

There are children who have been so hurt by their past experiences that they will go on having special needs throughout their childhood, even though they have clearly benefited from becoming a loved member of the family. If you adopt a child who is likely to have particular ongoing needs, you should ensure as far as possible that the agency will make arrangements for them to have any special help they may continue to require on a long-term basis.

---

*On a bad day I see the damage and wonder how I'll ever give enough, how I'll ever make enough of an impact to compete and triumph over the impact of the abuse that has robbed my daughter of years of her life and has the potential to rob her of her whole life…On a good day I know I am winning and feel I am the luckiest mother in the world.*

Adoptive mother, *Adoption Today*

---

## Groups of brothers and sisters

About half of all the children waiting for adoptive families are in groups of brothers and sisters needing to be placed together. Most of these children are in groups of two, although there are some groups of three or more. Brothers and sisters can provide support and comfort for each other throughout their lives. If they want to stay together and if an assessment of their needs has shown that one family could parent them successfully, it is very sad if they have to be separated because no families come forward for them all. You may be daunted by the practicalities, but extra help and support could and should be available (see Chapter 5). Brothers and sisters share a family history and can support each other in making sense of what has happened to them. Research indicates that, compared to children of the same age placed on their own, brothers and sisters placed together are likely to do as well or better.

---

*There can be rivalry and spats, and their perception sometimes is that they "hate" each other! But it's obvious that having each other is a tremendous reassurance. It is the only constant and stable thing they've had in their lives.*

Adoptive parents of three brothers, *Be My Parent*

---

## Disabled children

Disabled children may be placed for adoption at a very young age when their parents feel unable to care for them, or they may be looked after by the local authority after their parents have tried unsuccessfully to cope. So they may feel the impact both of their disability, the loss of their family of origin, and perhaps the confusion of a residential setting where different staff come and go. People who adopt these children will need to be prepared for a challenging yet rewarding task, as some of the children will never be able to lead entirely independent lives. In some cases, experience of disability in prospective adopters – either their own personal or professional experience or that of their children – will be positively welcomed.

---

*The other thing about adopting older children is that you know if there are any medical issues or developmental issues. A lot of the issues that affect children in care will be evident, whereas if they are a year old, you might not know.*

Adoptive parent, *The Pink Guide to Adoption*

---

## Learning disabilities/difficulties

There are many babies and older children who have learning difficulties/disabilities waiting for adoption, for example, children with Foetal Alcohol Spectrum Disorder. These are children who, as well as individual love and care, need additional help and support to enable them to participate in as many as possible of the experiences and opportunities open to any other child.

There are many children whose learning disabilities are not clear-cut: they may have suffered an accident or injury while very young which has affected their ability to learn or to understand the world around them – but no one knows how much. Or they may have been born with a disability that isn't clear to doctors. They may have been chronically neglected and/or abused as a baby and young child, and the extent of the damage this has caused and the possibility of change may still be unclear

---

*Our fourth birth child taught us not to be afraid of disability. She was born with Edward's Syndrome, and through this we became aware of the disabled children left in hospital because their parents found it too difficult to cope. So we decided to adopt.*

Adoptive mother of two disabled children, *Could you be my Parent?*

---

## Physical disabilities

There are many types of physical disability – cerebral palsy, muscular dystrophy, spina bifida and cystic fibrosis are just some of them. Children with these disabilities need the love and security that life in a family offers just as much as other children do. And, like most children, they will give love and affection in return. Having a physical disability does not mean having a learning disability too, although people sometimes confuse the two. People with physical disabilities can lead increasingly independent lives nowadays – especially if they have the support of a loving family.

# Are children from different ethnic backgrounds waiting to be adopted?

Yes, there are children from a great variety of ethnic, cultural and religious backgrounds waiting for adoption. They all need families who will cherish and value their heritage and identity; families who either match their ethnicity, culture, religion and language as closely as possible, or who can actively promote these aspects of their identity.

# Do the children all have contact with their birth families?

It depends on what is meant by contact. It can mean anything from an adoption where the child has regular face-to-face contact with members of his or her birth family to an adoption where the adopters have met the birth parents once and there is an annual letter exchanged via the adoption agency. Many children being placed for adoption now will have a plan for their adoptive parents to have at least an annual exchange of news with their birth family via the adoption agency. Others will need and want to meet members of their birth family, sometimes grandparents, brothers and sisters, and occasionally their parents, perhaps once or twice a year.

Contact must be planned to meet the child's needs. These will
change over time and everyone involved needs to be prepared to be
flexible. Contact can be very positive and can result in a child being
more rather than less settled in their new family. Contact can
sometimes be easier for everyone to manage if the child's adopters
match their heritage as closely as possible. You will need to be clear
what the plan for contact is for any child whom you plan to adopt.

---

*Our twin boys joined us when they were three…Direct
contact is planned with their other siblings twice a year. The
boys don't have memories of living with them so we are
going into the unknown, but so far their relationships seem
very positive. We talk about their siblings and have photos
around the home.*

Adoptive parent, *Be My Parent*

---

# 02

# Who can adopt?

*Adopters are needed from all backgrounds – it is for everybody. I don't have my own home, a lot of money or a partner but I do have time, energy and unconditional love for this little boy, my son. It's about having the capacity to take on the challenge.*

Adoptive mother, *Be My Parent*

## Are there long waiting lists for adopters?

No. It is estimated that well over 4,000 children looked after by local
authorities in the UK are waiting and could be adopted if enough
adopters came forward. They are children like those described in
the previous chapter and adopters, both couples and single people,
those with or without children already and people of various ages
are urgently needed to offer them a chance of family life. The only
group of children for whom there are more potential adopters than
there are children, are white babies without disabilities. Rather than
keeping waiting lists of people wanting to adopt only this group of
children, agencies may have their lists closed. They are able to place
these babies with adopters who are also interested in a wider range
of children.

## Do I have to be "special" to adopt?

No, but understanding, energy, commitment, and the ability to face
up to challenges and difficulties will all be needed.

Just as you will be providing support and understanding to a child
with a variety of different needs, so you will need support yourself.
Your family, including your children if you have any, plus your close
relatives and friends, need to be in agreement with your plan, because

---

*If your family isn't on your side from the beginning, the whole
process will be much more difficult. Even before the adoption
process starts, it's essential that the support network is there –
especially from your family...The child has to grow up with
your relatives, as well as you.*

Adoptive parent, *Be My Parent*

---

you will almost certainly call on them for help. Your immediate family will, like yourself, be very closely affected. Children who have been hurt by their experiences can hurt others in their search for security.

You will need all the help you can get. In return, though, you will get the joy and satisfaction of seeing some of the emotional damage to a child gradually start to heal. The rest of this chapter gives information on issues which you may be concerned or unsure about. The adoption agencies which you contact will also give you written information on their eligibility criteria for prospective adopters.

## Are there age limits?

You have to be at least 21 years old to adopt in law (unless you are a birth parent involved in a joint step-parent adoption, in which case the age is 18).

There is a greater health risk as people age. Agencies have a responsibility to ensure as far as possible that prospective adopters are likely to be fit and active at least until their child is a young adult. Although there is no upper age limit, many agencies would not usually expect there to be more than about a 45-year age gap between the child and their adoptive parents. However, this is flexible and depends partly on what the adopters are offering in relation to the needs of waiting children. The average age of adopters currently on referral to the Adoption Register for England and Wales is 43.

Birth mothers placing infants for adoption often ask for their child to be placed with parents within average childbearing ages. So, if agencies do take families on for babies for whom there is a huge choice of families, they may choose to work with slightly younger people.

---

*It's stating the obvious, but it's a fact: adoption changes your life! You can't just absorb a child into your family without changing your lifestyle. You have to give up certain things,*

*you have to make financial adjustments, you have to cope
with emotional pressures and deal with changing
relationships. I think we grossly underestimated the impact
adoption would have on our lives.*

Adoptive parent, *The Family Business*

## Do I have to be married?

No. Single people, both men and women, can and do adopt, as well
as couples.

The Adoption and Children Act 2002, implemented in England and
Wales in 2005, also enables unmarried couples, whether
heterosexual, lesbian or gay, to adopt jointly, as does the Adoption
and Children (Scotland) Act 2007, implemented in 2009. In Northern
Ireland, at the time of writing (October 2013), unmarried couples,
including same-sex couples and those in a civil partnership, can apply
to adopt jointly. However, this may be subject to change, so check
this information with your agency.

People who have been divorced can adopt. If you are married or
in a partnership, adoption agencies may prefer you to have been
together for a year or more before taking up an adoption application
from you.

## Do I have to be British?

No. You are eligible to adopt a child in the UK if your permanent
home is in the UK (the legal term is "domicile") or if you have been
habitually resident in the UK for at least a year. If you are adopting as
a couple only one of you needs to be domiciled or both of you need
to be habitually resident. Habitual residence is quite a difficult status
to define and you may need to take legal advice on whether you
qualify. You will need to be resident in the UK for long enough to be

assessed and approved as adopters, to have a child placed with you and to apply for the adoption order in court. This could take at least two years and possibly longer.

Most children needing adoption will already have had a number of moves. They are likely to be insecure and to need as much stability as possible. They may also have some ongoing contact with members of their birth family. For these reasons it may not be appropriate for many children to be placed with adopters who will be moving around a lot or living overseas after the child's adoption.

## What if I'm British but working abroad for a few years?

Unless you are making arrangements for the adoption of a child already well known to you, you will almost certainly not be able to adopt a child in the UK until you return to live here.

You usually need, for practical purposes, to be living in the UK for at least two years, so that the adoption agency has a chance to work with you and get to know you, and also to match you with a child and to introduce and place the child. This is followed by a period of at least ten weeks, before you can apply for an Adoption Order. It is not until you have an Adoption Order that you will be able to take the child to live abroad with you.

## What if I am disabled or in poor health?

Medical conditions or disability will not necessarily rule you out. All prospective adopters have to have a full medical examination done by their GP. The adoption agency employs a doctor who acts as a medical adviser. He or she will want your permission to contact consultants who have treated you. The adoption agency's prime concern is that you will have the health and vigour necessary to meet the needs of your child until he or she is a young adult.

## What about lifestyle issues like smoking?

There is evidence that smoking causes health problems for smokers and that passive smoking can damage the health of others, particularly young children. For this reason, many agencies will not usually place pre-school children with people who smoke.

Excessive alcohol consumption also leads to health problems. It may also be associated, for children in care, with violence and physical abuse. Your drinking habits will therefore need to be discussed with you.

There is also evidence that obesity can cause health problems as can anorexia or other eating disorders and so these conditions will be carefully considered by the agency.

## What if I've got a criminal record?

People with a record of offences against children or who are known to have harmed children cannot be considered by adoption agencies. A criminal record of other offences need not rule you out. However, the nature of the offence and how long ago it was committed will have to be carefully considered. It is important to be open and honest with the adoption agency early on if you have a criminal record. The information will come to light when the police and other checks are done and any attempt at deception by you will be taken very seriously. Criminal records checks will also be made for all members of your household aged 18 or over in England and Wales, 16 or over in Scotland and 10 or over in Northern Ireland.

## What about finances and housing?

You do not have to own your own home or be wealthy. Adoption agencies prefer there to be a spare bedroom available for a child. However, this isn't a legal requirement and an adopted child could share a bedroom with a child already in your family. Your child would obviously need to be happy about this and it would be helpful if you had a contingency plan in case the children really didn't get on with sharing. You may be eligible to receive financial support from the local authority in certain circumstances, such as if the child whom you wish to adopt has special needs and if you could not afford to adopt him or her otherwise. (Adoption support is described in more detail in Chapter 5.)

---

*We were enthusiastic and honest. We told her that we had had problems in our marriage and gone for counselling, and she was very positive about it.*

Jasminder, adoptive parent, *Looking After our Own*

---

## Does it matter if we're still having treatment for infertility?

You can certainly get written information from adoption agencies and also attend an information session or ask for an individual interview to find out about adoption. However, you will then need to decide whether to continue with infertility treatment or to pursue adoption. Adoption agencies will not usually be prepared to embark on a full adoption assessment and preparation with you while you are still actively involved in infertility treatment. It can be very difficult to pursue two different routes to parenting at the same time. Experience shows that most people need to end treatment and "mourn" the birth child whom they are not going to have before moving on to think positively about all the issues involved in adoption.

## We'd like to adopt a child the same age as our son/daughter so that they can grow up together

There is quite a lot of research evidence which shows that it is more likely that things will not work if a child joining a family is close in age to a child already there. Agencies, therefore, often prefer to have an age difference of two years or more between children. It is also often easier for your children and for the new child if he or she can join your family as the youngest child. However, it is possible for children to come in as the eldest or as a middle child, so do discuss this with the adoption agency if you feel it might work in your family.

## I'd like to be considered for children from any ethnic background

The Adoption and Children Act 2002 states that 'In placing the child for adoption, the adoption agency must give due consideration to the child's religious persuasion, racial origin and cultural and linguistic background.'

There are more white children than any other group needing adoption and so it makes sense for white families to adopt white children whose particular needs they can meet as fully as possible.

We have to accept the fact that racism is still common in Britain today. So black children – including those of mixed (black and white) heritage who will probably be identified as black – will, sooner or later, have to cope with some form of racism. A black child who faces racist abuse outside the home is likely to find it easier to discuss what has happened, understand it, and learn how to deal with it from a black adopter who can immediately relate to this experience. Coping with racism is something white people are not so geared to, whereas for black adults it is a fact of life. Black children need this level of support in their daily life.

Black children also need black adults they can look up to and with whom they can identify positively. For children who have been unable to stay with their own black families and who are then placed in white families, it can be hard to correct the false impression that white is better than black.

Matching ethnicity, religion, culture and language between a child and their adoptive family is likely to make it easier for the child to settle, may help facilitate any continuing birth family contact, and will have the long-term advantage of the child learning naturally and easily about his or her heritage.

Agencies are much more successful now at placing children with adopters who reflect their ethnicity. However, when this isn't possible without delay for the child, adopters will be sought who will cherish and value the child's heritage and identity and do all they can to promote it. This is likely to be easier for adopters who live in an ethnically diverse area and who have contacts with people who share the child's ethnicity, culture, religion and language of origin.

Guidance to the Adoption and Children Act 2002 states that:

> *A prospective adopter can be matched with a child with whom they do not share the same ethnicity, provided they can meet the child's other identified needs. The core issue is what qualities, experiences and attributes the prospective adopter can draw on and their level of understanding of the discrimination and racism the child may be confronted with when growing up.*

---

> *It doesn't really matter what other people think. I know who I am...I can say proudly that I'm half Scottish and half Indian and that my nationality is British and Australian and that I was raised by white, English parents...It always makes for an interesting conversation when someone asks me where I'm from and I now have the choice as to how much I wish to disclose.*

Adopted adult, *In Search of Belonging*

---

# I'm worried about an open adoption. Will this rule me out?

It depends what you mean by an open adoption. The term is used to mean anything from a one-off meeting with your child's birth parents and an annual exchange of news via the adoption agency to regular face-to-face contact between your child and members of their birth family. It is recognised now that it can be helpful for some children to maintain some face-to-face contact, perhaps with a grandparent or a brother or sister placed elsewhere and sometimes with their birth parents. Face-to-face contact is not the plan for all children and you can discuss with the agency your wish not to have a child who needs this to be linked with you.

However, *all* adoptive parents need to have an open attitude to their child's birth family and past. You need to recognise the importance of this for your child and be prepared to talk with your child about his or her often confused feelings about their birth family and their past. You also have to accept that things can change and that your child *may* want direct contact in the future even though that isn't the plan now.

---

*I perhaps sometimes don't really want to acknowledge the fact that he's adopted. I wish he was mine, my biological…so, yeah…but I'm very conscious that it's something that we need to be very open about, you know, so that he is prepared for the future and knows as much as possible.*

Adoptive mother, *Gay, Lesbian and Heterosexual Adoptive Families*

---

A one-off meeting with birth parents can be very valuable in helping you talk with your child about their birth family and it can be reassuring for the child to know that you have met his or her birth parents. Most adoption agencies would expect you to be prepared for a one-off meeting. They would also expect that you could consider at least an annual exchange of news, usually anonymously via the adoption agency, with your child's birth parents.

---

*If you are critical of the people who are part of your child's make-up, then you are rejecting part of them. But if you accept and empathise with the past then you can make a good life for your child. The gains are enormous.*

Adoptive mother, *Could you be my Parent?*

---

## Can I adopt my foster child?

This is discussed in Chapter 8.

## Can I adopt a member of my family?

The law in England and Wales, Scotland and Northern Ireland allows a child to be placed for adoption by a parent with the child's brother, sister, uncle, aunt or grandparent, without this needing to be agreed by an adoption agency.

For a child who is unable to live with his or her birth parents, living with a member of their extended family may well be the next best thing. However, there are other ways to give the child security which you could also consider. For instance, a Special Guardianship Order or a Residence Order gives the carers parental responsibility without taking this away from the birth parents and cutting the child off from them legally, as an Adoption Order does. If you are considering adopting a family member, you may find it helpful to talk this through with a social worker from the local authority where you live, before you apply. There is more information on Special Guardianship and Residence Orders in Chapter 8.

If you decide to go ahead with the adoption you can start the process for applying to court. The Adoption and Children Act 2002 for England and Wales requires that at least three months before applying to a court to adopt you must notify the social services department of the local authority where you live of your intention to apply. The Act also requires that the child must have lived with you for at least three years out of the last five before you apply. However, you can apply to court for permission to make an application sooner. You can apply to your local Magistrates' Family Proceedings Court, County Court or the High Court.

In Scotland you must also notify the Social Work Department of your intention to adopt. You would then petition the Sheriff Court. The child must have lived with you for thirteen weeks before you can get an Adoption Order.

The local authority must prepare a comprehensive report for the court. This will involve interviews with you, the child and the child's parents, who will need to consent to the adoption. Medical reports and checks will need to be done. Should the child's parents decide to withdraw their agreement at this stage, the court can consider dispensing with it, if there is compelling evidence to do so.

If a child in your family is already being looked after by the local authority and seems unlikely to return to his or her parents and you would like to consider offering the child a permanent home, you should contact the child's social worker or local authority as soon as possible. They will welcome your interest.

# 03

# How do I get approved to adopt a child?

*I used my assessment to analyse what I really wanted and I thought hard about how much I value the size of my own family. I decided I actually wanted to adopt siblings!*

Adoptive parent, *Be My Parent*

## First steps

It can be helpful to do some reading about adoption as it is today and about the sorts of children needing families before you approach an adoption agency. This book is a good start and other useful books and leaflets are listed at the end.

Many people thinking about adoption also find it invaluable to speak to experienced adopters. Adoption UK is a self-help group for adoptive and prospective adoptive parents before, during and after adoption. It has local groups throughout England, Scotland, Wales and Northern Ireland which you could join and whose members will be pleased to talk to you (see Useful Organisations).

If you live in England, you could also contact First4Adoption, a national contact point for information which includes e-learning material – www.first4adoption.org.uk.

## Contacting an agency

This important step is fully covered in Chapter 10, followed by a complete list of adoption agencies in England, Wales, Scotland and Northern Ireland.

## Can I respond to children I see featured in a family-finding magazine before I contact a local agency?

Yes, you can. Social workers featuring children in *Be My Parent*, *Adoption Today*, local newspapers and other media are happy to hear from unapproved families. However, their priority is to place their child with a suitable family as soon as possible and so they will follow up approved families first. However, if you are within their geographical catchment area they may well decide to take up an application from you. This might be because you are the most suitable (or the only!) family who has responded to their child. It might also be because they think that you are offering a valuable resource to a child, even if they cannot place the child to whom you have responded with you.

The child's social worker might ask an agency local to you to do the assessment on their behalf, if you live at a distance. Alternatively, he or she might suggest that you contact a local agency, as there are other possibilities for the child whom they have featured. As discussed in Chapter 10, you need to think carefully about being assessed by an agency a long way away as it may be difficult for them to offer you adequate help and support once you have a child placed with you.

---

*My daughter told us they were going to adopt. Next thing we heard was, they were going to adopt three together. Then they said they weren't going to be babies. We didn't like to ask too much but we didn't know what to expect or what was expected of us.*

Parents of adopters, *Related by Adoption*

---

## What will happen after I've contacted an agency?

The process described below was introduced in England in 2013. There will be some variations in Scotland, Wales and Northern Ireland, although the issues covered in preparation groups and in the assessment will be broadly the same.

### 1 Initial information gathering

Once you have contacted an adoption agency covering your area, they should respond within ten working days. They should invite you

# The adoption process (in England)

## Adopters

Contacting agencies and expressing an interest

Information meeting(s)

Registration of Interest

**Stage One – pre-assessment**

    Police, health and other checks

    Personal referees contact

    Some training and preparation

**Stage Two – assessment**

    Further training and preparation

    Work with an assessing social worker

    Prospective Adopter's Report (PAR) completed

Adoption panel recommendation

Agency decision

Search for a child

## Child

Statutory looked after child review

Adoption plan agreed

To adoption panel if parents agree to adoption

Agency decision on the adoption plan

To court if parents do not agree to adoption

Care order and placement order

Family finding

---

Matching meeting and report

Adoption panel recommendation

Agency decision

Placement planning meeting

Possible child appreciation day

Introductions

Placement

Review of placement

Adoption application

Adoption Order

to an information meeting or offer you an individual visit or a pre-planned telephone call. These can take place in the evening or at a weekend if this suits you best. You will be given information on the adoption process and on the parenting needs of the children. This is an opportunity for you to consider whether adoption is likely to be right for you and how adopting a child who may have a range of complex needs will impact on your family. If you decide to proceed to the next stage, you need to complete a Registration of Interest form which the agency will supply. Among other things, this will authorise the agency to undertake the checks described in the next section. It will also confirm that you have not registered with any other agency. The agency should decide within five working days from receipt of your form whether or not to accept it. If the agency lacks the capacity to undertake assessments in the immediate future, it should advise you of this and offer to refer you to First4Adoption (see Useful Organisations) or to another agency.

## 2 Stage One – the pre-assessment process

This stage begins when the agency accepts your Registration of Interest and should normally take no more than two months to complete. The agency should discuss with you the work which will take place and should complete a written Stage One agreement with you detailing this. It should offer you some initial training and preparation and it must also complete the prescribed checks.

Checks are made of criminal records for you and members of your household aged over 18. Offences other than specified ones, i.e. those against children, need not rule you out, although the nature of the offence and how long ago it occurred will need to be carefully considered. It's vital that you are open and honest. Any attempt at deception will be taken very seriously. These checks are made to the Disclosure and Barring Service (DBS). Checks will also be made of the local authority where you live. You will be asked for the names of at least three personal referees, people who know you really well, and they will be interviewed. If you have parented children with a previous partner, the agency will want your permission to contact him or her. They may want to talk to adult children whom you've parented. They will want to check that you are not seriously in debt and that payments on your home are up to date. Finally, you will need a full medical examination carried out by your GP. This will be considered by the adoption agency's medical adviser.

If the agency decides during or at the end of Stage One that you are not suitable to adopt, it must inform you in writing with clear reasons. You may make a complaint to the agency about this or raise concerns with First4Adoption. However, you are not able to apply to the Independent Review Mechanism. You may, if you wish, take a break of up to a maximum of six months after Stage One, or you may notify the agency that you wish to proceed straight to Stage Two.

## 3 Stage Two – the assessment process

This stage starts when the agency receives notification from you that you wish to proceed with the assessment process. It finishes with the agency decision about your suitability as an adopter and should normally be completed within four months. A Stage Two written assessment plan must be completed with you, detailing the assessment process, dates for meetings and agreed training. The social worker designated to work with you will visit you at your home. The purpose of these visits is for the social worker to gain a detailed view of you and other family members in the home, in order to assess your suitability to adopt a child.

Some of the issues which will be covered with you will be:

- your life history, and experiences of being parented;
- your relationships, past and present, with wider family, friends and partners;
- your personality and interests;
- your ethnicity, culture and religion;
- your reasons for wanting to adopt and your expectations;

- your parenting experience and skills;
- your openness towards birth families;
- your support network, using support and problem-solving skills;
- employment and finance;
- strengths and limitations.

The social worker will want to talk with your children, both those at home and usually with adult children living elsewhere. They will usually also want to meet an ex-partner with whom you have parented children. They may well want to talk further with your referees, although they will have had contact with them during Stage One of the process.

All adoption agencies are required to provide preparation and training and you will almost certainly be invited to a series of group meetings, often about six, of two to three hours each. You will be with other prospective adopters, usually about eight or ten people. As well as hearing from social workers about adoption and the children waiting, you will usually also hear from experienced adopters, an adopted adult and perhaps from a birth parent whose child has been adopted, about their experiences. You will have the opportunity to ask questions and to reflect on your own life experiences and on the impact of any adopted child on your family and how you will adapt to meet their needs.

---

*I sat in the car park for ages, trying to pluck up the courage to get out of the car. I don't know what I was scared of. Not being good enough, I suppose. Once I got in it was fine. Everyone was welcoming and they were a very diverse group of people. I had thought it would be all couples, all white, but there was a real mixture.*

Adoptive parent, *Looking after our Own*

---

The issues covered will include:

- why children need to be adopted;
- issues of loss, separation and trauma;
- how children become attached to their carers and the effect on them of the poor attachments which they are likely to have experienced;
- the significance of continuity and contact for children who are separated from their birth family;
- the sorts of behaviour which children who have been neglected and abused may display;
- the key parenting skills which are likely to be needed;
- support networks and support services.

---

*I found the training really informative. I know some people thought there was too much focus on negative things, but I didn't want the agency painting a glossy picture and then a child going back into care because I couldn't cope.*

Adoptive parent, *Be My Parent*

---

## What exactly are they looking for?

Social workers are looking for people who can make and keep close relationships, who are open and honest, able to talk about their feelings and about their limitations as well as their strengths; who are adaptable, flexible and willing and able to resolve and learn from difficult experiences; who enjoy children and are willing and able to put the child's needs first; who know that every child, even a tiny baby, comes with a past and a birth family who are important; and people with "staying power" and a sense of humour.

Although this process is thorough, searching and quite intrusive, many prospective adopters actually quite like the opportunity to reflect on their life and on their relationships and find it a stimulating and interesting experience. Often, a good and trusting relationship is built up with the social worker.

---

*It was good to talk about our plans for the future and to reflect on the past. You quite often forget the good things that have happened in the past but I remembered friendships I formed as a child and how I used to play. It helped me to get into the framework of looking at things from a child's perspective.*

Adoptive parent, *The Pink Guide to Adoption*

---

## What can I do if I have concerns at this stage?

If you are concerned that adoption, at this stage in your life, may not be right for you, you should discuss this with your social worker. You can, of course, withdraw from the process at any point. It is much better to be open about any doubts or concerns that you have at this stage rather than waiting until you are linked with a child.

You may still be keen on adoption but, as happens occasionally, be finding it difficult to work with your social worker. You need to try to share your concerns with your worker but if you can't resolve things between you, you could consider contacting their manager for help. It is possible, although quite unusual, to have a change of worker part-way through the process.

You can, of course, withdraw your application from that agency at any point. However, if you apply elsewhere you may well have to start again from the beginning. The second agency will also need to contact the first one for any comments which they may have. You should be able to see anything which is put in writing (provided it doesn't include third party information, for example, from your referees).

## Fast-track approval process

This is available to anyone who is an approved foster carer in England and to people who have previously adopted in a court in England or Wales under the Adoption Agencies Regulations 2005 (or Welsh equivalent). If this applies to you, you will be able to enter the adoption approval process at Stage Two. Agencies are required to complete the process within four months.

## The assessment report

A written report will be compiled, with your help. You must be given a copy of the report to read, apart from the medical information, checks and information from your personal referees (which remain confidential to the agency). You have five working days under English regulations in which to comment, in writing if necessary, on anything that you disagree with the social worker about or that you think should be added. BAAF's Prospective Adopter's Report (PAR) (England) is widely used by agencies in England.

---

*The whole home study business is like opening a Pandora's box and this person takes you on a journey through issues you've never analysed before. Unless you feel safe with the social worker, it could be tempting to cover things up.*

Adoptive parent, *Be My Parent*

---

## The adoption panel

The report is presented to the agency's adoption panel for their recommendation. This is a group of up to about ten people, including social work professionals, a medical adviser, and independent members, who are people with knowledge of and an interest in adoption. These almost always include at least one adoptive parent and an adopted adult. The regulations about membership of panels are different in England and Wales from Scotland, but their purpose is the same: to consider prospective adopters and to make a recommendation to the agency about whether they are suitable to adopt or not.

You must be invited to attend the panel, or at least part of it, if you wish. Most prospective adopters do attend. Most are very nervous beforehand but find the actual experience less daunting than they thought. Panel members find it extremely helpful to meet prospective adopters and to have the opportunity to have a brief discussion with them.

The panel may consider and give advice to the agency about the number, age range, sex, likely needs and background of children whom you could adopt. However, it is the agency which makes the final decision on this.

Occasionally the panel will defer making a recommendation, pending additional work being done or information gathered. You will need to clarify exactly what is being asked for and by when.

## The final decision

After the panel has made its recommendation, a senior officer in the agency considers whether or not to approve you as an adopter. In England and Wales, if the agency is proposing not to approve you, they must write to you first giving you their reasons and asking for your comments. In England, applicants at this stage have 40 working days within which to make comments (representations), either to the decision maker or to the Independent Review Mechanism (IRM) (see below), but not to both. In Wales, applicants have 40 working days to apply to the Independent Review Mechanism Cymru (see below). In England, Wales and Scotland, the agency must write and tell you their final decision, whether it is approval or non-approval. It should be unlikely for you to get to this stage and not be aware of any concerns about you from your social worker. The vast majority of people who get to this stage in the process are approved as adopters.

---

*It's been great to meet so many people going through the same process we are, and all having arrived at the same point.*

Adoptive parent, *Frozen*

---

## A brief report

Occasionally social workers will decide, before they have completed the assessment, that they will not be able to recommend you as suitable to adopt. They will discuss their concerns with you and you will have the option of withdrawing from the process. However, if you decide that you want to proceed, the social workers can write a brief report which, in England, is then treated in the same way as a full report, i.e. you must see it and can comment on it, it will go to the panel and then to the decision maker. If the decision maker proposes not to approve you, you will have the right to apply to the IRM in England or Wales (provided that your agency is in one of these countries).

## Independent Review Mechanism (IRM) England

This is run by BAAF under contract to the Department for Education. It is only available to people assessed by adoption agencies in England. If you receive written notification from the agency, following a panel, that it proposes not to approve you (or to terminate your approval), you can apply to the IRM. You must do this within 40 working days. The IRM will arrange for your case to be heard by an independent IRM panel, which you can attend. The IRM panel will make a recommendation which will go to your agency. The agency decision maker will then make the final decision.

## Independent Review Mechanism Cymru

This is run by BAAF under contract to the Welsh Assembly and is available to people assessed by adoption agencies in Wales. It operates in a very similar way to the IRM in England.

## What happens if I'm not approved?

If the agency has not been able to approve you, you should discuss with them fully the reasons why. They will have been disappointed not to be able to approve you and will have thought about this very carefully and so you may agree with them that perhaps adoption is not for you. However, you can, if you wish, approach other adoption agencies and start again. Sometimes, people turned down by one agency are approved by another and go on to adopt successfully.

If you feel that the service that you have had from the agency has been poor you can, if you wish, make a formal complaint about this to the agency.

## Do I have to pay the agency?

There is no charge for the home study, assessment and preparation if you are adopting a child who is in the UK. However, if you are asking an agency to do a home study so you can adopt a child from abroad, they will probably make a charge (see Chapter 7).

# How long will it all take?

This process, from your Registration of Interest to approval by the agency, should not usually take more than six months. This is the timescale in the Guidance to the Adoption and Children Act for England. National Care Standards for Scotland suggest a similar timescale of around seven months.

However, the Guidance does recognise that there may be "exceptional circumstances" which mean that the agency needs to take longer or, of course, you may want or need to take longer. You may want more time to think things over or to prepare your children or other family members or there may be events in your life which mean you need to take a short break. You should talk this over with your social worker.

# 04

# How do I find a child?

*Actually, it's not so much the waiting...it's the not knowing how long you will have to wait that really frustrates you.*

*The hardest part of the adoption process is...the bit after all the euphoria of actually being approved to adopt a child.*

Adoptive parent, *Frozen*

## What happens after approval?

Once you have been approved as suitable to adopt a child, the agency must prepare a written matching agreement with you, setting out the matching process and your role in identifying a possible child for placement with you.

If you have been approved by a local authority, they will consider you carefully for their waiting children or for a child from the local consortium of agencies to which they may belong. Unless a link with a specific child is being considered, the local authority must, with your agreement and within three months, refer you to the Adoption Register for England and Wales for active consideration for children referred to the Register, or to the Adoption Regional Information System (ARIS) if you are in Northern Ireland, or to Scotland's Adoption Register.

If you have been approved by a voluntary adoption agency, they will help you to find a waiting child. They will encourage you to respond to children in *Be My Parent*, *Adoption Today* and other media, and they will probably agree to refer you to the Adoption Register or ARIS straightaway. (See Useful Organisations for more information on the Registers and on ARIS.)

## Considering possible children

Your agency may approach you to discuss a possible child or you may respond to a child whom you see featured as needing a new family. You will probably talk with your own social worker first and with the child's social worker. You will also be given written information about the child. You will then meet the child's social worker and also, perhaps, their foster carer. It is important, in the excitement of hearing about a possible child at last, that you take time to consider the child's needs carefully and how you will be able to meet them. You may want to follow up particular issues with the social workers or the foster carers or with a doctor, or check whether the necessary services, for example, special schooling, are available in your area. It is important that you have as much information as possible about the child and their background. Your social worker has a responsibility to ensure that you receive this and should help you consider it.

---

*It is a learning process and we are working out how to filter the information more efficiently. It is hard to reject children but you have to be realistic, you have to weigh up what the child needs and what you can offer.*

Adoptive parent, *The Pink Guide to Adoption*

---

The child's social workers may still be considering other families at this stage. They should keep you and your social worker in touch with what is happening. If they decide that another family has more to offer this particular child, they should try to explain this to you.

## Fostering for Adoption (FFA)

New regulations which came into force in England in July 2013 allow an agency to give an approved adopter temporary approval as a foster carer for a named child. This enables a child to be placed as a foster child with carers without them having had a full fostering assessment or panel approval as foster carers. These will be children for whom the likelihood of eventual adoption is high. However, the child is fostered until, in most cases, work with birth parents and court involvement enables an adoption plan to be agreed and the child to be matched for adoption with these carers at panel. If you might be interested in becoming an FFA carer, you should discuss this with your agency during your assessment. The children placed in this way are likely to be quite young. However, there is a risk that, for some reason, adoption is not agreed as the plan or court involvement takes longer than anticipated.

## Concurrent planning

See Chapter 8.

## Being matched with a child

The Adoption Agencies Regulations for England introduce fairly detailed requirements for this part of the process. Arrangements in other parts of the UK will be broadly similar but not identical.

Once the child's social workers have decided that you seem to be the right family for a particular child and you are also keen to proceed, they must give you a copy of the child's permanence report (a comprehensive report about the child, comparable to your assessment form). They must also give you any other reports and information on the child's health, education or special needs which would be helpful. They should meet with you to discuss all this, including the plans for any post-placement contact for the child with birth relatives or others. If you and they are keen to proceed, they should then assess what adoption support you and the child will need.

The social workers should then write an adoption placement report which should include the proposed contact and support arrangements. You must be given 10 days to read and comment on this.

This report plus your assessment form and the child's permanence report will be presented to an adoption panel, usually the one in the child's local authority. Your social worker and the child's social worker will attend and you will also be invited to attend. It can be extremely helpful to the panel if you can do so.

As with your approval as an adopter, it is a senior officer who makes the decision about the match, based on the recommendation of the panel.

It is unusual that matches are not agreed at this stage, although it can happen. Occasionally recommendations and decisions are deferred if the panel or agency require more information. There is no formal appeal process if a match is turned down.

## What support and help will be available?

It is very important that you discuss with both the child's social worker and with your social worker at this matching stage, what sort of support and help you and the child will need after placement. As described above, there should be a written plan, discussed and agreed with you, about this. It should cover any special arrangements which need to be made to meet the child's educational and health needs and any therapy which may be needed. It should also cover the support and help which will be available to you. If you will need financial help, the necessary means test should be done and an agreement made as to the level and frequency of any payments.

One adoptive parent, if in employment, is entitled to statutory adoption leave for one year. The Statutory Adoption Pay rate is currently £136.78, or 90 per cent of average weekly earnings, whichever is the lower, and is paid for the first 39 weeks. The other parent, if there are two, if employed, is entitled to two weeks' statutory leave at the same rate. To qualify for either, you must have completed 26 weeks continuous service with your employer up to the date of matching.

## What is a child appreciation day?

Some, but not all, agencies arrange these days. They invite all the key people who have known the child, such as former foster carers, teachers and relatives, to meet with you. This enables you to build up a really detailed and "living" picture of the child and their life so far.

*I think you're so nervous about meeting the people because you know they've chosen you because they think you're better. I mean they've looked through a whole catalogue or magazine…and seen you and thought that's who they wanted. So you feel nervous about meeting them. You think, 'Well, am I going to be good enough?'*

Adopted girl, *Adopted Children Speaking*

## Introductions and moving in

Once a decision has been made about a match, the social workers will meet with you to confirm plans for support, for contact with the birth family, for your exercise of your parental responsibility and for introductions. They will work out with you and with the child's foster carers a plan for introducing you and the child to each other. Introductions may be daily for a week for a young baby, or rather more spaced out over a longer period for an older child. They do not usually last more than six to eight weeks though.

Many adopters prepare a little book for the child with photos of themselves, their pets, their house, etc, and some prepare a short video or DVD. These are then shared with the child by their foster carers prior to the first meeting. Most foster carers are skilled at preparing and supporting children to move on, although it is an emotional time for them, as well as for you and the child.

You should discuss any doubts or concerns that you may have with the social workers during this period. If you really do not feel that the match is right, it is much better to say so at this stage rather than later.

*Don't underestimate how difficult it is on the day you have to take them from the foster carer's house…Everybody was standing around – the social worker, the foster mum and dad and us – and we had to put them in the car…Suddenly he was saying, 'You are making me move again…I'm losing my friends…I don't understand my life…This isn't fair, everybody just leaves me.' We were all crying.*

Adoptive parent, *The Pink Guide to Adoption*

# 05

# What happens after a child moves in?

*When he first moved in I found it so difficult and now I look back and I'm astonished at how hard I found it 'cause now, it's not always easy – I used to think I was very tolerant and patient and I'm not, I'm intolerant and very impatient [laughs], which is a bit sad 'cause it can affect your view of yourself, but I think we've got a very good relationship.*

Adoptive mother, *Gay, Lesbian and Heterosexual Adoptive Families*

Your child or children moving in is only the beginning. Adjusting to a different way of life will take time and there will be difficult periods. You and your child may well need help and efforts are being made to ensure that this is available.

## Parental responsibility

The Adoption and Children Act 2002 gives adoptive parents in England and Wales parental responsibility on placement, rather than just on adoption, as formerly. You will share this with the child's birth parents and with the local authority which is placing the child with you. The local authority must discuss with you, before they place the child, whether they propose to restrict your exercise of your parental responsibility in any way. You could agree, for instance, that they will still be involved in decisions about visits abroad or health treatment. Once the child is adopted you have exclusive parental responsibility with no restrictions.

## What help will be available?

It is important, as described in the previous chapter, to talk to your social worker and to the social worker for your child, before the child moves in, about the help and support and special services which may be necessary. You should, if you are adopting in England, have a written Adoption Placement Plan, which has been discussed and agreed with you. This should cover support arrangements as well as arrangements for contact with the birth family, and for the exercise of your parental responsibility. If appropriate, referrals should already have been made for specialist therapy or educational or health services which your child may need. This will be especially important if you are adopting an older child who may have experienced considerable trauma, or a child who has suffered from neglect or abuse. In such cases, access to appropriate help will be crucial.

Social workers from the adoption agency which assessed and approved you, as well as from the child's agency, if different, will offer you all the help they can during the settling-in period. They are required to visit at regular intervals and to review how things are going. Adoption UK also offers invaluable support and help to adoptive families, and there are local groups throughout the UK.

## Will there be any financial help?

You should be clear before the child moves in about any practical and financial support which can be given. Many local authorities pay a settling-in grant, especially if you are adopting older children, which could be several hundred pounds, to cover your initial outlay on equipment such as beds and car seats. If you are adopting a group of brothers and sisters, it is possible for them to pay towards, for example, a larger car and for equipment such as a large washing machine. Regular financial support – an adoption allowance – may be available for certain children, a group of brothers and sisters, for example, or a child with disabilities or with serious behavioural difficulties. This regular financial support is means tested but you should enquire about this if you think you need this help at any stage. There is an annual paper review of your means, which determines the level of the financial support.

---

*Joe liked the feeling of living in chaos. Chaos was familiar to him. He still sometimes preferred the old feelings he recognised to the new feelings of calm and contentment.*

Adoptive parent, *Together in Time*

---

# Will support be available after adoption?

Many adoption agencies now have "after adoption" or "post-adoption" workers. They keep in touch and offer the opportunity to talk over issues. They also often organise group events on subjects such as managing difficult behaviour or talking to children about adoption. They can also help you access specialist services which you and your child may need. Much of the UK is also served by After Adoption or Post-Adoption Centres, which exist to help familes. Adoption UK can also provide valuable support from other experienced adopters. Efforts are currently being made to try and improve services around the UK for adoptive families.

---

*I couldn't have done it without any of them. Some have been "all rounders", while I've put others into categories; for instance, the person who is brilliant with practical support but brushes emotional things under the carpet. But every single person has played a part in helping me.*

Adoptive parent, *Be My Parent*

---

Adoption Support Services Regulations for England make it clear that adoptive families have the right to request and be given an assessment of their adoption support needs, including the need for financial help, at any stage in the child's childhood. The responsibility for this assessment stays with the local authority which placed the child for three years after the Adoption Order. After this, the responsibility for the assessment moves to the local authority in which you live. There are also regulations in relation to support in Scotland, and published policies in Northern Ireland.

The Adoption Passport, available from First4Adoption, gives information about the kinds of post-adoption support that may be available, the statutory provisions that already exist and those which may be introduced if the Children and Families Bill being debated in Parliament in late 2013 becomes law, possibly in 2014.

## What about the birth family?

Birth parents whose children are adopted usually find this a hard and painful experience. Occasionally they have requested adoption, but usually the decision has been made by others, sometimes much against their own wishes. However, they are often still important to their children and many of them are prepared to co-operate with the adopters and the agency in offering what they can to their child.

It is usually to the benefit of the child if the adopters can meet the birth parents at least once and continue to exchange basic information about the child. This is usually through the adoption agency which acts as a "letterbox" for a letter perhaps once a year. It is now recognised that maintaining some level of contact can be of benefit to children as they grow up and helps the adopters answer questions about the birth parents, what they were like, where they are now, and so on. Ongoing contact will not be right in all cases and will need to be handled sensitively.

---

*I think it's important, I think it will be important to him as an adult. I don't think it's important to him now particularly. I think in a way he'd prefer not to think about it or not to talk about it…but I understand its purpose and I think when he's older he will appreciate those letters.*

Adoptive father, *Gay, Lesbian and Heterosexual Adoptive Families*

---

For some children visits may continue after adoption. This may be with birth parents or with grandparents and other significant adults or it may be with brothers and sisters who are living elsewhere, perhaps in other adoptive families. Older children may know where their relatives are living and want a family who can help them keep in contact. Again, this is something that you, the agency, and the child, if old enough, will need to discuss and agree on well before the adoption goes through to court. However, it is important to remember that the child's needs and wishes will change over time and you do need to be prepared to be flexible.

---

*We have annual letterbox contact with our son's birth mother. It's hard work building up to it – I wonder each time what to say, how his birth mother will picture him from the letter and photos…It tears me to shreds, writing a letter once a year. There's a huge sense of relief afterwards. But at the same time I feel overwhelming love for him. It doesn't upset me to send the letter, but brings me that feeling of love.*

Adoptive mother, *Could you be my Parent?*

---

## Why do children have to know they are adopted?

Many children who are adopted were old enough when placed to remember something of their past and so they obviously know about their adoption. However, all children have the right to know about their past. Increasingly, it has been acknowledged that an open rather than a secretive attitude is more helpful to the child. After all, there is always the danger that someone else will tell the child without any warning, or perhaps in a hostile way, for example, in a family row. Finding out like this can be a terrible shock to a child who may well wonder what else you have concealed from them.

Even older children may be very confused about what happened in the past. They may blame themselves for the things that went wrong in their birth family. So it is important to be honest and to discuss adoption quite naturally, right from the start.

From the age of 18 in England, Wales and Northern Ireland, and 16 in Scotland, adopted children have the right to their original birth certificate if they want it – although their adoptive parents may already have given it to them.

The BAAF book, *Talking about Adoption to your Adopted Child*, can help you with the kind of issues you will face (see Useful Reading).

This is when the information collected by the adoption agency about the child's birth parents and early life, often in a life story book, will be needed. Children who are not given any facts sometimes have fantasies about their circumstances or history and may well believe the worst, so it is kinder and fairer to tell them the truth. This is not something that you do just once. Children need to go over their story again at different stages in their growing up, understanding a bit more each time.

---

*You go through a phase of reading his life story book, like, most evenings for maybe a week or so, and then nothing again for another month or six weeks or something like that.*

Adoptive mother, *Gay, Lesbian and Heterosexual Adoptive Families*

---

## Social networking websites and contact

Social networking websites such as Facebook have had a huge impact on the way that people communicate with each other. Finding and contacting people is much easier than ever before, with both positive and negative outcomes.

It is important that you are aware of the way in which the use of the internet, social networking and other technologies such as smartphones are changing the whole context of adoption contact. You need to know what you can do to protect privacy and security in the best interests of your child. However, you also need to recognise that there is a limit to how far you can control and monitor the use of these new forms of contact by your child and/or members of their birth family. You may need to manage complex situations which arise from unauthorised and unmediated contact.

## What if the adoption doesn't work out?

Some adoptions do go wrong – like marriages, they do not always work. The first few weeks and months can produce problems that no one anticipated so there is always a settling-in period of at least three months and usually considerably longer, before an Adoption Order is made. Of course, the social worker from the agency will keep in touch with you and will help and support you as much as possible. If you feel that things really are going wrong during this period, and that you cannot continue with the child, you owe it to yourself and to the child to tell the agency.

Once the adoption has been made legal, the child will be legally yours just as if you had given birth to him or her. The sources of help described above will be available. If the problems cannot be resolved, the Social Services or Social Work Department can take responsibility for the child again. However, the adoptive parents will remain the child's legal parents until and unless the child is adopted again by new parents.

It is estimated that about 20 per cent of adoptive placements come to an end. The child's age at placement is one of the major factors, with the risk increasing the older the child is at placement.

---

*Adoptive families should be trusted and treated as responsible parents unless there are concerns about safeguarding the children. Above all else, when adoptive families are in a state of crisis, they must be taken seriously! Their views need to be heard, their perceptions have to be taken into account and their pain has to be acknowledged.*

Adoptive parent, *Adoption Undone*

---

## What will happen to the child if things don't work out?

If the child does have to leave, he or she will go either to a foster family or possibly to a residential home. If it isn't possible to resolve the difficulties with you, another adoptive home may be found, but the difficulties that arose between you and the child will have to be understood to try and prevent the same thing happening again. Usually, agencies arrange a meeting, called a disruption meeting, which enables everyone concerned to come together and reflect on events and what can be learned from them. Sometimes the problems arise when the child is much older, 16 plus, and like many teenagers, is having difficulty feeling at home in a family setting. The best solution then may be to support the child in an "independent" setting such as lodgings. He or she may well value having you around to advise and reassure him or her even if living together is too difficult at that point in their lives.

---

*Things are very good for my daughter…we have put a lot of work into supporting her and trying to draw her back into the family after some nightmare years…so far, so good…and we love her to smithereens…that's all we have left after being brought very low over a long period of time…the love.*

Adoptive mother, *Facing up to Facebook*

---

## Could I try again?

You may feel you and the child were not right for one another, and that you could succeed with a different child. If the social worker agrees with you, you may get the chance to adopt again. After all, different children need different families and just as a second attempt may work for a child, so it may work for a family. You could apply to the same agency again or to a different one. You would need a further period of assessment and preparation and the adoption panel and the agency would need to consider whether or not to approve you again to adopt.

# 06

# How is adoption made legal?

*I love reading the ending of a book because of the feeling of triumph that you've finished it...and I guess that was the same feeling in court, watching them close the book, really shutting it...Knowing that nothing else was going to happen. It was just going to be an ordinary life from now on.*

Adopted girl, *Adopted Children Speaking*

When you adopt a child, you become the child's legal parent. The child usually takes your surname and can inherit from you just as if he or she was born to you. All responsibility for making decisions about the child and his or her future is transferred to the adopters. An adoption is not legal without an Adoption Order made by a court. Once an Order has been made it is irrevocable and cannot be overturned.

## How do I get an Adoption Order?

You have to apply to court for an Adoption Order. You apply in England and Wales to your local Magistrates' Family Proceedings Court, to a County Court which deals with adoption (now a network of designated adoption centres), or to the High Court; in Scotland you lodge a petition in the Sheriff Court or the Court of Session; in Northern Ireland you apply to the County Court or to the High Court. Your adoption agency should be able to help you with the process and the court. You will need to obtain an application form from the court and complete and return it. If you are not adopting a child who is looked after by a local authority, you will also need to notify the Social Services or Social Work Department in your area of your intention to adopt at least three months before you apply to court. They will have a duty to visit you and your child and to prepare a report for the court.

## When can I apply to court?

The Adoption and Children Act for England and Wales requires that if your child has been placed with you by an adoption agency, he or she must have lived with you in the 10 weeks before you make the application to court. If your child is older or has special needs, you will probably want to wait longer and give yourselves a chance to settle down together properly before applying to court. You will need to discuss with your social worker when the right time would be to apply to court. There are different timescales for relatives, step-parents and others adopting a child who has not been looked after and placed by an adoption agency. These are detailed in the relevant chapters. In Scotland and Northern Ireland, the child must have lived with you for at least 13 weeks before an Adoption Order can be made, if placed by an adoption agency.

## What happens before the court hearing?

Before the court can consider your application, it will require a social worker from the local authority which placed your child with you, or from the one where you live if your child was not placed by a local authority, to prepare a report. It is a detailed report which includes information about your child and their birth family, about you and about the placement, both the reasons for it and also how it is going. In Scotland, an independent person appointed by the court called a curator *ad litem* will prepare a report. In England and Wales a Children's Guardian may be asked by the court to prepare a report in some cases. These workers will need to talk with you and your child, as well as with the birth parents.

## What happens in court?

Adoption hearings are usually very short if the child's birth parents are in agreement, and in Scotland you may not need to go to court. You need not expect it to last more than half an hour, and you should be told at once whether the Adoption Order is granted. A report will have been prepared for the court which the Judge, Magistrates or Sheriff will consider. You will probably be asked some questions, and so will the child, if he or she is old enough. The Judge must consider the views of the child, taking account of the child's age and understanding. Also, in Scotland, any child of 12 or over is asked formally if he or she consents to the adoption. The only reason to dispense or do away with the child's consent is if he or she is incapable of consenting. Many courts try to make the occasion as relaxed and celebratory as possible.

---

*Adoption is sad and happy at the same time because you get a new family but you can lose one too. Being adopted does not mean you have to miss out on anything – and sometimes you get extra.*

Adopted child, *Finding our Familia*

---

## What if the birth parents don't agree?

In England and Wales, a local authority must have authorisation to place a child with you before it can do so. This authorisation is either formal, signed consent by the child's birth parent(s) or it is a court order, called a Placement Order or a Freeing Order. (Freeing Orders can no longer be applied for, but existing ones remain in force.) Once this authorisation has been given and the child has been placed with you and you have applied to court, it will only be in exceptional cases that the birth parents will be able to contest the adoption and they will need the leave of the court to do this.

In Scotland, and in non-agency placements in England and Wales, if the birth parents do not agree, the adopters have to ask the court to override their wishes. The court can only do this in appropriate circumstances, for instance, if it judges that the parents are unreasonably refusing to agree. Cases like this are known as contested adoptions and if you are involved in one you will almost certainly need legal help. You should be able to obtain help with the costs, either through public funding (formerly legal aid) or from the adoption agency, and it is worth finding out about this at an early stage.

## What is a Freeing Order?

Before the Adoption and Children Act 2002 was implemented in December 2005, adoption agencies in England and Wales could apply to court for a Freeing Order for a child, either because the birth parents wanted to agree to adoption early, or because the agency wanted a court to deal with the issue of their consent early in the process. Freeing orders can no longer be applied for but existing freeing orders remain in force. Freeing is still used in Northern Ireland.

In Scotland, a Permanence Order is available for children who cannot live with their birth families. This order gives some parental responsibilities and rights to foster carers, and leaves some responsibilities and rights with appropriate people, including the child's parents, if that is in the child's best interests. This order will provide flexibility to adapt to a child's changing circumstances. Parental rights can be permanently removed.

## Are there any other legal issues?

Yes, a few, but if, as is likely, you are adopting through an adoption agency, it will usually sort things out for you. You can only receive a child for adoption in this country if he or she is placed by a UK adoption agency or via the High Court, unless the child is a close relative. Remember that any other private arrangement to adopt is *illegal*.

---

*Three years later and here we are settled together as a family! I have my nightmare days, heartaches, fears and frustrations, but then the children will come out with something really funny, and all is well again! I take the rough with the smooth.*

Adoptive parent, *Be My Parent*

---

## Will my child get a new "birth certificate" when he or she is adopted?

Yes, your child will be issued with a new short certificate in your name which looks the same as other short birth certificates. If you wish, you can apply for a long "birth" certificate, which will give your names and your child's new name. It will have "Copy of an entry in the adoption register" printed on it.

## What about legal fees?

If the birth parents do not agree to the adoption and decide to oppose it in court, it may get so complicated that you need a solicitor and a barrister if in England and Wales, or an advocate in Scotland. This means legal costs can rise, in some cases, to several thousand pounds. But you may be able to claim public funding – it depends on your income – or the local authority responsible for the child will usually pay most, or all, of the legal costs involved.

There is a fee for the court application but many local authorities will pay this when you are adopting a child for whom they are responsible.

---

*Being adopted means that when I grow up and have kids, my Dad and Pop can look after them.*

Boy of 6 adopted by a gay male couple, *Proud Parents*

---

# 07

# What about adoption from abroad?

*If you cannot accept the culture, customs, food, weather, people or any other aspect of another country then please do not consider adopting from there. That country is going to be part of your life for evermore and you need to support your child in developing a positive self-image based on their birth culture.*

Adoptive father of two children adopted from overseas, *Finding our Familia*

Some families are moved by the plight of children who have been the victims of war or natural disaster, or who have been abandoned in orphanages, and come forward to offer a home to such children. Others who may not be able to adopt in the UK the child whom they feel able or want to parent, may also seek to adopt from another country. In some cases, families may want to adopt a child who is a relative and lives in another country.

## Where can I get advice and help before deciding on this?

You can approach your local Social Services or Social Work Department. There is also a helpline run by the Department for Education and another run independently by the Intercountry Adoption Centre. Adoption UK will be able to talk to you about adoption generally and OASIS (Overseas Adoption Support and Information Service) will be able to help you with some of the issues particular to adoption from abroad. Written information is available from all these agencies and from BAAF (see Useful Organisations and Useful Reading). Many of the issues that you will need to consider are also relevant to adoption in the UK and are covered in Chapter 2.

## Surely adoption overseas is the best plan for children living in extreme poverty?

It may be the best plan for some children in the short term. However, children have the right to remain in their own community and their own country, if at all possible, and countries overseas are working to this end. They need help from more affluent countries, and from individuals in those countries, to achieve this. In some countries, the "loss" of their children to overseas adoption has triggered the development of adoption services, and programmes to improve child care services have been launched, sometimes in collaboration with or funded by child care services from more "developed" countries.

The numbers of adoptions from overseas has remained fairly stable over the last few years at around 150 per year. This is a lower figure than previously, as countries overseas develop their own adoption services.

## Wouldn't countries in crisis welcome this sort of help?

In an emergency, it is impossible to gather the information needed to make a decision about whether the child really needs adoption. For example, are the child's parents alive or not? They may be in hospital, in prison, in hiding or refugees in another country, and may re-emerge to claim their child later. Intercountry adoption is not a suitable way of dealing with the needs of children who are moved as a result of war, famine, or other emergency. Indeed, many of these children will be emotionally damaged by abandonment, malnutrition, the effects of war, and separation from their families. In a crisis, the child needs to be made safe in as familiar an environment as possible. Experienced aid workers find that the vast majority of children separated from their families by war or other emergency can be reunited with relatives when the crisis recedes. What is required is temporary care in a secure and loving environment, not the permanence of adoption.

*What was she going to become? How had her parents managed to survive all the hardship and famine?...She was a mystery: her roots, her genetic make-up – everything was hidden from us. It was a case of what we saw was what we got.*

Adoptive parent, *From China with Love*

# I really only want a child without health problems

There can be no guarantee about this when you adopt from abroad.
There is often very little information available about the child's early
experiences and medical history or that of their birth parents, all of
which will have implications for the child. Depending on the country
of origin, the child may have been exposed to the risk of conditions
such as tuberculosis, HIV infection, hepatitis B and C. Reliable and
safe testing may not always be available. The child may also have
suffered considerable physical, emotional and intellectual deprivation
which may have long-term effects. Other factors, for example, the
likelihood of any inherited conditions, will probably never be known
until they manifest themselves.

## What is the process for adopting from overseas?

You must have a home study done by the Social Services or Social
Work Department for the area where you live or by an approved
voluntary adoption agency which is also approved as an intercountry
adoption agency. It is *illegal* to commission a private home study
report. Many of the issues which will be covered in the home study
are the same as those discussed in Chapter 3. The assessment
process is similar, including the involvement of the adoption panel. If
your adoption agency is in England or Wales you will also have the
option of applying, if necessary, to the IRM or IRM Cymru.

---

*Our daughter, Amy, has a serious congenital hearing loss
which we didn't know about when we adopted her from
China. We love her and we are coping, although we'd always
said that we didn't want to adopt a child with a disability.*

Adoptive parent

---

When the adoption agency has approved you as suitable to adopt from your chosen country, the home study report is sent to the Department for Education, the Scottish Government, the National Assembly for Wales or the Northern Ireland Department of Health, Social Services and Public Safety depending, of course, on where you live.* It is they who will then endorse the application.

## Is the whole process expensive?

Yes, it certainly can be. Most local authorities in the UK, whose first priority must be the placement of children whom they are already looking after, make a charge for the home study to cover their costs. Charges can range from £4,000 to £6,000 or more. There will also be the cost of travel at least once, or possibly more often, to the child's country. Documents need to be translated, there are usually lawyer's fees and charges made by the agency overseas.

In addition, the Department for Education charges applicants in England and Wales a fee for its part of the process. This is currently £1,775. However, there is a means test and applicants wishing to adopt a close relative from overseas will be exempt.

## How do I decide which country to apply to?

The home study must be in relation to one country only and it is for you to decide which one. It is likely to be helpful if this is a country with which you already have links or can make links. It will be important for your child that you have knowledge and understanding of the culture, religion and history of the country and, if possible and realistic, some knowledge of the language. You will need to know, or be prepared to get to know, adults from the country who are willing to play a part in your child's life. It can also

* In the rest of this chapter Department for Education should be read as including the other equivalent bodies.

be helpful to have contact with other families who have adopted
children from that country.

## How will I be linked with a child?

The process described here is that for England and Wales. You
should enquire locally about the slightly different process in Scotland
or Northern Ireland. Once the adoption agency has decided on your
suitability to adopt and the Department for Education has endorsed
the application, the latter will send all your papers to an agency in
the country you have chosen. The authorities in the child's country of
residence will decide whether to accept your application, and having
done so, your name(s) will be placed on their waiting list for a child.
It is the responsibility of the authorities in the child's country of
residence to match a child with you.

When the authorities overseas have identified a child for you, they
will send you some information about the child including some
medical details. The amount of information provided varies greatly.

When you have received this information, it will be important to
discuss it with your own GP and you must also discuss it with your
social worker. The agency medical adviser may also be able to give
you advice. BAAF's leaflet, *Children Adopted from Abroad: Key
health and developmental issues*, will also be useful.

When you have made the decision to go ahead with the proposed
match, you will need to make arrangements to travel to the child's
country to meet the child. If you are then happy to proceed with the
adoption, you must notify your adoption agency of this in writing.

## How do I have the child placed with me and bring
him or her back to the UK?

The arrangements for this will vary according to the adoption laws
and procedures of your chosen country, whether the country has

ratified or acceded to the Hague Convention and whether or not it is on the UK's list of designated countries. You will need to comply with the requirements of the child's country as well as with UK immigration requirements. Your adoption agency and the other sources of information already described will be able to advise you.

## Will I have to adopt the child again in the UK?

As described above, this will depend on the country which your child comes from and the arrangements made for the placement in that country. It will be necessary in some situations to apply to adopt to a UK court once you have returned here with the child.

## What support will be available after I adopt?

The adoption agency which does your home study should discuss with you what support they can offer after adoption. There are post-adoption centres in England and Wales which can help you and there are also two main support groups of adoptive parents, Adoption UK and OASIS (see Useful Organisations). There are also groups of adopters who have adopted children from particular countries. Adoption UK, OASIS or the Intercountry Adoption Centre should be able to give you information on these.

## I would like to adopt a child overseas who is related to me

If there has been a crisis in your extended family overseas and, for instance, a child's parents have died suddenly, you can apply for that child to join you in the UK as a dependant. You need to apply to the nearest British diplomatic post in the child's country. If it is agreed that the child has no other family locally able or willing to care for the child, and that the child needs to join you, entry clearance to the

UK and indefinite leave to stay may be granted. Once the child has settled with you in the UK, you can decide whether or not adoption would be a good idea.

However, it may be that a relative overseas is planning to help you in your wish to be a parent by giving you one of their children, or you may wish to adopt a child in your extended family overseas who is living in poverty or difficult circumstances. The process in this situation would be to apply to an adoption agency here for a home study, as described earlier in this chapter, but to check out at the same time, through the British diplomatic post in the child's country and the immigration authorities here, whether entry clearance would be likely to be granted. It is unlikely that it would be granted for a child who is being "gifted" to you. Adoption has to be about meeting the needs of a child who is unable to live with their birth parents or other local relatives and who needs to be adopted.

# 08

# What about fostering?

*I enjoy working with the adults as much as the child. If I had my own children and I was at home with them all day, it would drive me mad. But you go to meetings and get involved with the plans and decisions and you're always working towards things. It's brilliant.*

Foster carer, *Growing up in Foster Care*

# What is fostering?

Fostering is a way of providing family life for someone else's child in your home. Most of the children looked after by local authorities when their own families are unable to care for them are placed in foster families. There are roughly 62,000 children in foster care in the UK, just over 65 per cent of all looked after children. Families are unable to care for their children for a variety of reasons. Sometimes parents have poor physical or mental health and have to be hospitalised, or they may abuse drugs or alcohol and need help to overcome their addiction. Children may have been neglected and they may also have been abused.

 Local authorities work with parents to make plans for the children. Their parents may have asked for them to be looked after, or a court may have ordered that a local authority should share responsibility with their parents. In Scotland, a Children's Hearing may have made a supervision requirement, with a condition that the children reside with foster carers. Also, in Scotland, the court may grant a Permanence Order to the local authority giving them almost all parental responsibilities and rights and the local authority may have the child looked after by foster carers.

# What about the foster child's parents?

Fostering is shared caring. Foster carers are not the child's legal parents and do not have parental responsibility. They usually share the caring with the child's birth parents, as well as with the local authority. Being a parent whose child is in foster care is painful, and foster carers need to understand this and be sympathetic. Although they are not living with them, their parents are usually important to children who are fostered. They often want to see them or courts may order this, and parents will have a big part to play in making plans for the children's future. It is estimated that 70 per cent of children who are looked after return home within a year.

*To begin with, we thought we had to protect him from all the goings on in his family. Then we realised he knows more than he lets on and it's better to have it all out in the open.*

Foster carer, *Ten Top Tips for Supporting Kinship Placements*

Children in foster care can be visited by their parents in the foster home or have contact in a neutral venue, supervised by a social worker. Sometimes part of the task is helping the parent learn to care for the child. Other relatives, like brothers or sisters or grandparents, may also keep in touch with the child.

## Could I foster a baby?

You can say which age children you would prefer to foster and, if you prefer to look after babies or small children, you should say so. But it is important to remember that fostering is not a way into adopting a baby or young child. You will be expected to care for the child on a short-term basis until he or she returns home or until other plans are made.

*We just love having children around. We've got a grown-up daughter and two teenagers at home and we also foster. We like having groups of brothers and sisters and we've got three at the moment. They're aged two, four and five and their social worker has just found adopters for them which is great, although we'll miss them!*

Foster carer

## Fostering and adoption

The majority of fostered children are able to return to their birth families. Many children need help for only a few days or weeks, but others may stay for months or even several years while permanent plans are made and carried out. For some children, adoption becomes the plan and foster carers have an important role in helping the child to move on to their new permanent family.

Fostering does not usually lead on to adoption. You have to get used to seeing a child leaving your home, a child you have grown to love. But it can be very satisfying – children who arrive frightened and upset can leave feeling much more confident. Helping a child move on is one of the most important tasks of foster carers.

---

*I knew she only acted like that because that was the way she'd been treated herself. So we decided to keep her, because she'd had a rough deal – and she deserved a chance.*

Jane, foster carer, *Foster Care*, issue 25

---

Sometimes, however, there might be agreement between social services and yourself that it would be best for a particular child to remain with you or be adopted by you. This would need full and careful discussion and you would need to be re-assessed and approved as an adoptive parent. Currently in England, just over 350 children a year, or nine per cent of all the looked after children adopted, are adopted by their foster carers. A survey in Scotland found that almost a third of children needing a permanent new family found this by remaining with their foster carers, some through adoption and others through long-term fostering.

If you have fostered a child for a year or more and you want to adopt, it is possible to notify the local authority of your intention to adopt and to apply to court for an Adoption Order. However, it is much better to work with the local authority if you can.

In Northern Ireland, adoptive applicants are sometimes approved as foster carers and adopters, and will foster the child pending resolution of the court freeing process.

## Fostering for Adoption

See Chapter 4.

## Concurrent planning

This is the term given to a small number of schemes currently operating. Children, usually babies or toddlers, for whom there is one last chance that they might return home to their birth family, are placed with families who will foster them with this aim. However, the foster carers are also approved as adopters and will adopt the child, should the planned return home not be successful. In this way, the moves that a child may otherwise have to make are minimised. These schemes operate with the agreement of the local court and to tight timescales.

Families who have children placed under a concurrency scheme have to be prepared to facilitate very regular contact for the child with their birth family and to be prepared that the child may return home. However, adoption often becomes the plan for these children and the carers can then adopt a child who has been placed with them from a young age. If you might be interested in becoming a carer in a concurrency scheme, First4Adoption or BAAF will be able to tell you which agencies operate such schemes.

## What about long-term fostering?

Sometimes, particularly for children aged 10 or over, foster care may be the plan until the child grows up. This long-term fostering cannot provide the same legal security as adoption for either the child or the foster family, but it can be the right plan for some children.

Some older children may accept, reluctantly, that they will never be able to return home to live and that they need a new family. However, they may be clear that they do not want to be adopted. They may also need a lot of extra help, for example, special schooling, hospital appointments, regular therapy sessions. You may decide that you would like to work in partnership with the local authority to offer long-term fostering to a child or young person. The child would remain the legal responsibility of the local authority and of their birth parents. For some children in Scotland, the local authority will have obtained a Permanence Order, giving it almost all parental responsibilities and rights.

You would receive a regular fostering allowance as well as being able to call on the local authority for help and support. You need to understand that many of the children for whom long-term fostering is the plan are at least nine or 10 years old.

## What kind of people become foster carers?

Many different kinds of people are able to give children a loving and secure foster home. Some foster carers have young children of their own; some are older people whose children are now young adults; others may not have any children of their own. Some are couples and others are single. Some people foster one child at a time, others more than one; some foster only babies or toddlers, others particularly like to look after teenagers. Foster carers come from all walks of life and live in all kinds of homes. It is the job of the social worker in the local authority or child care agency to find the right foster carers for each child, and this includes considering cultural and religious factors, among others.

## Would I get paid?

Yes. The fostering allowance covers the cost of feeding, clothing and looking after the child. Fostering allowances vary from area to area and according to the age and needs of the child. Sometimes, foster carers are paid more than just their allowance for looking after a child. They can be paid a fee in recognition of their particular skills and/or because the child whom they are fostering has special needs.

## How would I go about fostering a child?

First of all, you need to contact a fostering agency covering your area. This could be your local Social Services Department (England and Wales) or Social Work Department (Scotland) or Health and Social Services Trust (Northern Ireland). It could also be a neighbouring one although, as children are usually placed as close as possible to their home area, it is a good idea to apply to an agency as close as possible to where you live. You need to ask to speak to someone in the fostering team.

Voluntary organisations and independent fostering agencies also recruit, assess and approve families for fostering.

Details of all fostering agencies are on BAAF's website and in the BAAF book *Fostering a Child*.

*Throughout the assessment we were treated as individuals, it focused on what we'd done before, the strengths we might have to look after children, as well as the difficulties.*

Justin and Dan, foster carers, *Recipes for Fostering*

## How would I get approved to foster?

Most agencies run preparation and training groups for prospective foster carers as well as meeting with you individually. The whole family will need to be involved. If you have birth children, they will need a chance to think about what fostering will mean for them. Confidential enquiries will be made of your local authority and the police and you will probably be asked to have a medical examination. The fostering agency to which you have applied will prepare a report, with your help, on your application. This report is presented to the agency's fostering panel, a group of up to ten people, who include social workers and independent members and at least one foster carer. You should be invited to meet the panel if you wish. The panel makes a recommendation on your application and this goes to a senior manager in the agency who makes the final decision. This process usually takes several months. National Standards in Scotland suggest that it should not take more than six months from the completion of the application form.

---

*Getting the training in managing difficult behaviour was a big help. We had this lad who was – I don't know, up and down all the time. Like a pot boiler. After the training I had these new ideas and more confidence, and some of them really worked for him!*

Barry, foster carer

---

## What if I'm not approved or if my agency wants to terminate my approval later on?

In this situation, you have a similar right to that of a prospective adopter to apply for an independent review of the proposed decision. You can apply to the Independent Review Mechanism (IRM) England if you live in England, or to the Independent Review Mechanism Cymru if you live in Wales. (See Chapter 3 for more information on the IRM.) The process is much the same as for adopters, except that you have to make the application within 28 days.

# What support would I get?

The fostering agency must make a foster care agreement with you when you are approved. This covers expectations of both parties and includes the requirement, laid down in regulations, that you should not administer corporal punishment.

As a foster carer, you have to work closely with the child's social worker as well as with the child's birth family. In the early stages this will ensure that you know as much as possible about the child, his or her likes and dislikes, normal routine, favourite foods and toys, etc. Later you will need to discuss the child's progress regularly with the worker and help plan for his or her future.

The local authority must keep records of foster children and foster carers. The local authority and foster carers must make a foster placement agreement, when a child is placed, about matters such as the arrangements for the child's health needs to be met, contact with the birth family and financial support for the child. The local authority must provide foster carers with written information about such things as the child's background, health, and mental and emotional development.

As well as having regular visits from the social workers for the children whom you are fostering, you will have your own supervising social worker, who is there to support and help you in the fostering task. Foster carers are also offered regular ongoing training and there may also be a programme of social events where you and your family can meet other foster families. There are formal Training, Development and Support Standards in England and a similar commitment to the support and training of foster carers in other parts of the UK.

The children whom you foster will have regular reviews, a month after placement, three months after that and then at least every six months. You will be involved in these and your input will be important. All foster carers are also required to have their approval reviewed every year and this provides an opportunity for you to comment on the support you have had.

*I see training as part of my support and I accept that I need all
the help that I can get to be able to do my job properly and
get the most enjoyment out of it.*

Foster carer, on Children's Workforce Development Council
(CWDC) website

## Special guardianship

This order was introduced under the Adoption and Children Act 2002,
from 30 December 2005 in England and Wales. In terms of legal
security it fits between adoption and a Residence Order. Birth parents
do not lose their parental responsibility and so there is still a legal link
between the child and them. However, the special guardian acquires
parental responsibility which they are able to exercise to the exclusion
of others with parental responsibility in all but a very few instances (for
example, agreement to a change of name or to adoption).

Special guardians whose child was looked after by the local authority
before the order was made are entitled to ask to be assessed for a
range of support services, including financial support. These support
services are very similar to those available to adoptive parents.

Special guardianship is seen as being appropriate when a child or
young person and their birth parents do not want to lose the legal link
between them but where it is agreed that the child needs permanent
new parents who will make all the day-to-day decisions about their
care and upbringing. It may be more appropriate than adoption in
some situations where children are being permanently cared for by
relatives. Special guardianship orders can be revoked by a court and so,
while giving more legal security than a Residence Order or long-term
fostering, do not give the complete legal security of adoption.

If you are a foster carer and think that special guardianship might be
appropriate, you should talk to the child's social worker and/or to a
solicitor with experience of child care law.

The process for applying is to notify the local authority in writing of your intention. Three months later you can apply to a Magistrates' Family Proceedings Court, the County Court or the High Court, provided the child has lived with you for at least one year. The local authority is required to prepare a report for the court. You should ensure as far as possible that your support needs are fully discussed and agreed at this stage, although you can apply for these to be further assessed after the order has been made, if necessary.

The BAAF leaflet, *Special Guardianship*, provides more information (see Useful Reading).

---

*I did not want to adopt my own grandchild...Remember, this is family...So guardianship seemed to be a nicer way of going forward and provided a bit more control for us.*

Grandparent, *Special Guardianship in Practice*

---

## Residence Orders in England and Wales and Northern Ireland

The making of a Residence Order under the Children Act 1989 or Children's (NI) Order 1995 gives people looking after a child more day-to-day rights than foster carers have, but not as many as adopters or special guardians. The child is no longer looked after by the local authority but the birth parents are still legally involved. They retain their parental responsibility but the holders of a Residence Order acquire this too. Foster carers can apply for a Residence Order even if the child's parents or local authority are not in agreement, provided that the child has lived with them for at least 12 months in England and Wales and for three years in Northern Ireland. The local authority can pay a Residence Order allowance, but is not obliged to do so. A Residence Order usually lasts until the child is 18 in England and Wales, and until 16 in Northern Ireland. If you want to know

more about Residence Orders you should talk to your local Social
Services Department or a solicitor with experience of child care law.

## Residence Orders in Scotland

In Scotland, anyone, including foster carers, can apply for a
Residence Order under section 11 of the Children (Scotland) Act
1995, if they can show that this is in the child's interests. A Residence
Order gives the carers parental responsibilities and rights but not as
many as an Adoption Order would and without removing all the
birth parent's responsibilities and rights. A Residence Order lasts until
the child is 16. The local authority can pay a residence allowance but
is not obliged to do so. Your local Social Work Department can tell
you more about the orders.

## Private fostering

Some parents make private arrangements for their children to be
looked after by private foster carers who are not approved and
registered with the local authority in the same way as the foster
carers described in the rest of this chapter. There are special
regulations for private fostering (see the BAAF leaflet, *Private
Fostering*, listed in Useful Reading).

## Further information

BAAF has a companion book to this one, *Fostering a Child*. This
would probably be helpful for you if you think that fostering rather
than adoption may be right for you.

# 09

# Stepchildren and adoption

*When my husband and I divorced, Jordan was only one-and-a-half and continued to live with me. A few years later I remarried and David and I had Julia. We really wanted the four of us to be a family. David wanted to adopt Jordan but, after talking this through with Jordan, who still saw her father regularly, we realised that this would not be right for her. We are now thinking of applying for a Residence Order.*

Birth parent

# ENGLAND AND WALES

You are a stepfamily if you or your partner have a child from a previous relationship who is living with you. It is estimated that more than 10 per cent of dependent children in England and Wales live in a stepfamily at any one time. Only a very small proportion of these children are adopted each year, about 900 children.

Most stepfamilies don't adopt. The adults involved work out satisfactory arrangements for the care and upbringing of the children, who will often have contact with the family members with whom they are not living. However, if you are considering adoption, the following information may be helpful. You may also want to read the leaflet *Stepchildren and Adoption* (see Useful Reading).

## Are there other ways to help make the child secure in our family?

### A parental responsibility agreement or order

The Adoption and Children Act 2002, which came into force in 2005, introduced this option for step-parents. It is available to a step-parent who is married to, or has entered into a civil registration with, the child's birth parent. A step-parent may acquire parental responsibility for the child by a simple but formal agreement with the parent who is his or her partner and with the other parent if he or she has parental responsibility. The agreement must be recorded on an official form and signed by each parent with parental responsibility and the step-parent, in front of a court official. Copies must be lodged at the Principal Registry of the Family Division. The official form and guidance notes can be obtained from the Court Service at www.hmcourts-service.gov.uk.

If the non-resident parent who has parental responsibility will not enter into this agreement an application can be made for a Parental Responsibility Order to a Magistrates' Family Proceedings Court, the

County Court or the High Court. There is no need to give prior notice to the local authority but the court may ask for a report about the child's welfare.

A parental responsibility agreement or order does not take parental responsibility away from parents who already have it.

### A Residence Order (see Chapter 8)

This is a court order which sets out with whom the child is to reside (or live). It also gives the step-parent who acquires it parental responsibility for the child. However, it doesn't take parental responsibility away from anyone else who has it, for example, the child's mother or the non-resident father if the parents were married when the child was born or if he has acquired parental responsibility. In effect, the child would have three parents with responsibility for ensuring his or her welfare. A step-parent does not need to be married to, or in a civil partnership with, the child's parent before applying for a Residence Order. You can apply for a Residence Order to your local Magistrates' Family Proceedings Court, the County Court or the High Court. It wouldn't prevent you applying for an Adoption Order at a later stage if you wish.

It is also important for the parent with whom the child is living to make a will, appointing a guardian for the child in the event of his or her death. If the step-parent is appointed and has a Residence Order, the child will stay with him or her should their birth parent die.

## We'd like the child to have the same surname as us

You don't have to adopt the child to achieve this. If the child's parents were married or the father has acquired parental responsibility, the child's surname cannot be changed without the agreement of the non-resident parent, unless a court gives permission. However, if the

child's parents were not married and the father does not have
parental responsibility, the child's surname can be changed with the
agreement of his or her mother either by common usage or by a
statutory declaration or by deed poll. You should consult a citizen's
advice bureau or solicitor about this. Obviously your child's wishes
should be taken into account. Many children now live in families
where there are a number of different surnames and they may be
quite happy with this and want to retain their own birth surname.

## Does the child's other parent have to be contacted and agree to an Adoption or Residence Order?

If the other parent is the mother, or is a father who was married to
the child's mother or who has acquired parental responsibility, his or
her agreement to an Adoption or Residence Order is necessary. A
court considering an application can dispense with the parent's
agreement but would need compelling reasons to do so. If the child's
birth father was not married to the mother and does not have
parental responsibility, his formal agreement is not necessary.
However, the court would want to know what his views were and
would usually require efforts to have been made to seek these. The
court would consider the father's views in relation to the part he has
played, or wished to play, in the child's life.

## Does the child have to know what is happening?

Yes. The court will want to know what the child's views are. This
would apply to children of three or so, and older. The court would
want assurances that younger children will be told the truth about
their parentage and about the adoption. This should usually start
from when the child is about three, so that they grow up always
having known.

## Do we have to be married before the step-parent can adopt?

No, the Adoption and Children Act 2002 no longer requires the step-parent to be married to their partner. However, they must have been living with them and the child for at least six months. The step-parent can apply for an Adoption Order and, if granted, this will give him or her the same parental rights as their partner, the resident birth parent, while taking away the parental responsibility and rights of any parent or other person who previously had this.

## What is the process for applying to adopt?

You must notify the local authority where you live of your intention to adopt. It can be useful to arrange to speak to a social worker in Social Services to discuss whether adoption will be a good plan. If you decide to go ahead, you must wait three months after notifying the local authority of your intention and then you need to apply to a local Magistrates' Family Proceedings Court, to a County Court or to the High Court. There will be a fee to pay and you will need to complete an application form. The court will require a social worker in the local authority to produce a full report for the court hearing. This will involve interviews with you both, with your children and with the other parent and this process should start once you notify the local authority of your intention to apply to adopt. On the basis of this report, the court will decide whether or not to make an Adoption Order. This process need not take longer than about three months, but can often take up to a year, depending on the circumstances of the case and the workload of the Social Services Department and the court.

## SCOTLAND

The situation is similar in that most stepfamilies do not adopt. As in England and Wales, a Residence Order can be a good alternative and can give the child some security and the step-parent considerable responsibilities and rights. There are some differences in the law and in procedures in Scotland.

## Change of name

There is a procedure whereby you can apply to change a name through the local Registrar's Office. You have to show that the child has been known by that name for at least two years. Your local Registrar's Office can help you with this.

## Your child's views about adoption

The law requires that the child's wishes and feelings are taken into account, as in England and Wales. However, in Scotland a child of 12 or over will be asked formally if she or he consents to the adoption.

## Do we have to be married before the step-parent can adopt?

No, the Adoption and Children (Scotland) Act 2007 allows a step-parent to adopt on his or her own, with the consent of the resident birth parent.

## Is the consent of the non-resident birth parent necessary?

Yes, if this is the mother or a father who has parental responsibilities and rights. If such a birth parent is in disagreement with the adoption, then the court can be asked to dispense with that agreement. There will need to be a proof hearing before the Sheriff. In this situation you would be well advised to use a solicitor.

## What is the process for applying to adopt?

Petitions are usually lodged with the local Sheriff Court. You also have to notify the local authority where you live that you intend to apply for an Adoption Order. When the court receives your application, it will appoint a curator *ad litem*, an independent person, who will meet with you and your child and prepare a report for the court. A social worker from your local authority will also visit you to discuss the application and will prepare a separate report for the court.

## NORTHERN IRELAND

With the consent of a non-resident birth parent with parental rights and responsibilities, a step-parent may adopt, but must do this jointly with the child's resident birth parent, to whom he or she must be married.

# 10

# Finding an adoption agency

*Picking up the phone the first time to admit to someone in authority that we wanted to adopt was surprisingly hard. I felt nervous – it was like nothing else I'd ever done before.*

Adoptive parent, *The Pink Guide to Adoption*

# Do I have to go through an adoption agency?

Unless you are a close relative of the child you want to adopt, you must apply to an adoption agency. There are over 200 adoption agencies in England, Scotland, Wales and Northern Ireland. Most of these are based in local authority Social Services Departments in England and Wales or Social Work Departments in Scotland. In Northern Ireland, social services are provided by Health and Social Care Trusts. These are listed in the following pages under the name of the county, borough or council, or Health and Social Care Trust.

There are also voluntary adoption agencies: Barnardo's is an example. Some of these are linked to churches, for example, the Catholic Children's Society. On the whole, all agencies work with applicants of any religious faith or none.

Local authority adoption agencies covering large areas tend to take applications mainly from people within their area. However, agencies which are geographically small, for example, London boroughs, often prefer not to recruit adopters from their own area as they will tend to live too close to the birth families of the children who need placement.

Voluntary adoption agencies usually cover a wider area than the local authorities do, often covering several counties. So it is worth contacting voluntary adoption agencies in counties near to your own, as well as any in it.

You are not limited to your own immediate locality, but most agencies work roughly within a 50-mile radius of their office. It is important to remember that you and your child will need help and support from the agency after placement. It is much harder for an agency to give you adequate support if they are based a long way away and you should discuss what their plans are for this before you decide to work with them.

## Would it be best to apply to the local authority or to a voluntary adoption agency?

Voluntary agencies tend to be small and to specialise in adoption and fostering work. They are often able to give very good support once a child is placed with you. Local authorities are bigger and have to respond to a wide range of needs. However, they are the agencies responsible for placing children and will usually consider families whom they have approved first. They may expect you to wait for up to three months after you are approved for the placement of a child looked after by them before referring you to an Adoption Register or consortium and before you respond to children from other local authorities whom you may see needing a new family. Voluntary agencies will actively help you to try and find a child, through using an Adoption Register or consortium, *Be My Parent* or *Adoption Today* and other contacts. So, there can be advantages and disadvantages in working with either type of agency.

## What they are looking for

All the adoption agencies listed in the following pages are looking for permanent new families for single children, particularly those of school age; for groups of brothers and sisters; and for disabled children and those with learning difficulties. There are children from a huge variety of ethnic, religious and cultural backgrounds.

## British Association for Adoption & Fostering

The British Association for Adoption & Fostering (BAAF) has close links with the adoption agencies listed in this book. You are welcome to contact BAAF for advice about the adoption process and about finding an agency. However, it does not take up adoption applications itself. There are several regional and country BAAF offices in the UK, and the contact details of these are included on the following pages.

If you live in England, you could also contact First4Adoption, a national information service on adoption in England (see Useful Organisations).

## How to find an adoption agency

On the next few pages, you will find lists of local authority and voluntary agencies in England, Scotland, Wales and Northern Ireland. These are divided into five different groups; each of these is served by BAAF offices located in that area.

When you have found the name of one or more agencies that are reasonably near you, you can phone or write for further information. Agencies may also have a website which you can visit. Guidance to the Adoption and Children Act 2002 states that you should expect to receive written information in response to your enquiry within five working days (seven in Scotland). You can contact a number of agencies at this early stage. However, you can make a firm application and enter into the preparation and assessment process with only one agency.

Unfortunately, we have not been able to include particular details about each of the agencies, for example, whether the agency occasionally needs families for white babies or whether it has a religious interest. A phone call to the agency will of course give you the necessary details. Your BAAF centre will also be able to help you.

BAAF's website enables you to find information about agencies covering your area – visit www.baaf.org.uk/res/agencydb/index.shtml.

First4Adoption also has information on all adoption agencies in England on its website at www.first4adoption.org.uk.

## BAAF CENTRAL & NORTHERN ENGLAND

Dolphin House
54 Coventry Road
**BIRMINGHAM**
B10 0RX
*Tel: 0121 753 2001*
*Email: midlands@baaf.org.uk*

Unit 4
Pavilion Business Park
Royds Hall Road
Wortley
**LEEDS**
LS12 6AJ
*Tel: 0113 289 1101*
*Email: leeds@baaf.org.uk*

and at

MEA House
Ellison Place
**NEWCASTLE UPON TYNE**
NE1 8XS
*Tel: 0191 261 6600*
*Email: newcastle@baaf.org.uk*

## LOCAL AUTHORITY AGENCIES

**BARNSLEY METROPOLITAN BOROUGH COUNCIL**
Adoption and Fostering Unit
Civic Hall
Eldon Street
**BARNSLEY**
S70 2JL
*Tel: 01226 775876*
*Email: adoptionandfostering@*
*barnsley.gov.uk*
*www.barnsley.gov.uk*

**BIRMINGHAM CITY COUNCIL**
Birmingham Adoption and Fostering
Service
PO Box 16262
**BIRMINGHAM**
B2 2WX
*Tel: 0121 303 1010*
*Email: vivien.meadows@*
*birmingham.gov.uk*
*www.birmingham.gov.uk*

**BLACKBURN WITH DARWEN COUNCIL**
Adoption Team
Children's Services Department
Link 3B
The Exchange
Ainsworth Street
**BLACKBURN**
BB1 6AD
*Tel: 0800 328 6919*

*Email: familyplacement@blackburn.
gov.uk*
*www.blackburn.gov.uk*

## BLACKPOOL BOROUGH COUNCIL

Children and Young People's
Department
Targeted Services
Progress House, Clifton Road
### BLACKPOOL
FY4 4US
*Tel: 01253 477888*
*Email: fostering.adoption@
blackpool.gov.uk*
*www.blackpool.gov.uk*

## BOLTON METROPOLITAN BOROUGH COUNCIL

Family Placement Team
Castle Hill Centre
Castleton Street
### BOLTON
BL2 2JW
*Tel: 01204 337480*
*Email: iwanttoadopt@bolton.gov.uk*
*www.bolton.gov.uk*

## BRADFORD CITY METROPOLITAN DISTRICT COUNCIL

Adoption and Fostering Unit
35 Saltaire Road
### SHIPLEY
West Yorkshire
BD18 3HH
*Tel: 01274 437343/331*
*www.bradford.gov.uk*

## BURY METROPOLITAN COUNCIL

Higher Lane Centre
Higher Lane
Whitefield
### MANCHESTER
M45 7FX
*Tel: 0161 253 6868*
*www.bury.gov.uk*

## CALDERDALE COUNCIL

Fostering and Adoption Team
Carlton Mill

Wharf Street
Sowerby Bridge
### HALIFAX
West Yorkshire
HX6 2AS
*Tel: 01422 256053*
*www.calderdale.gov.uk*

## CHESHIRE WEST AND CHESTER COUNTY COUNCIL

Permanency, Planning and Recruitment
Team
3rd Floor
4 Civic Way
### ELLESMERE PORT
CH65 0BE
*Tel: 0151 337 6492*
*Email: steve.smith2@cheshirewest
andchester.gov.uk*
*www.fosteringwestcheshire.co.uk*

## COVENTRY CITY COUNCIL

Social Services Department
Adoption and Fostering Recruitment
Team
Civic Centre 1
Little Park Street
### COVENTRY
CV1 5RS
*Tel:024 7683 2828*
*Email: family.placement@
coventry.gov.uk*
*www.coventry.gov.uk*

## CUMBRIA COUNTY COUNCIL

Children's Services Department
1–5 Portland Square
### CARLISLE
CA1 1QQ
*Tel: 01539 713312*
*www.cumbria.gov.uk*

## DARLINGTON BOROUGH COUNCIL

Children's Family and Learning
Fostering Team, Central House
Gladstone Street
### DARLINGTON
Co Durham

DL3 6JX
*Tel: 01325 388077*
*Email: pam.norgrove@*
*darlington.gov.uk*
*www.darlington.gov.uk*

## DERBY CITY COUNCIL
Children and Young People's
Department, Fostering and Adoption
Perth Street
Chaddesden
### DERBY
DE21 6XX
*Tel: 01332 718000*
*Email: adoption@derby.gov.uk*
*www.derby.gov.uk*

## DERBYSHIRE COUNTY COUNCIL
Derbyshire Adoption Service
County Hall
### MATLOCK
DE4 3AG
*Tel: 0800 083 7744*
*Email adoption@derbyshire.gov.uk*
*www.derbyshire.gov.uk*

## DONCASTER METROPOLITAN BOROUGH COUNCIL
Adoption Team
Civic Office
Waterdale
### DONCASTER
DN1 3BU
*Tel: 01302 737366*
*Email: adoption@doncaster.gov.uk*
*www.doncaster.gov.uk*
*www.adoptingindoncaster.org*

## DUDLEY METROPOLITAN BOROUGH COUNCIL
Directorate of Children's Services
Adoption Team
7th Floor, Falcon House (East Wing)
6 The Minories
### DUDLEY
*DY2 8PG*
*Tel: 01384 815891*
*Email: adoption.cs@dudley.gov.uk*
*www.dudley.gov.uk*

## DURHAM COUNTY COUNCIL
Durham Resource Centre
Fostering and Adoption
Littleburn Business Centre
Mill Road, Langley Moore
### DURHAM
DH7 8ET
*Tel: 0191 370 6100*
*Email: adoption@durham.gov.uk*
*www.durham.gov.uk*

## EAST RIDING OF YORKSHIRE COUNCIL
Adoption Team
Child Care Resources
Room BF64, County Hall
### BEVERLEY
HU17 0JT
*Tel: 01482 396673/6*
*Email: adoption@eastriding.gov.uk*
*www.eastriding.gov.uk*

## GATESHEAD BOROUGH COUNCIL
Adoption Team
Gateshead Council
Civic Centre
Regent Street
### GATESHEAD
NE8 1HH
*Tel: 0191 433 6388*
*Email: adoptionandfostering@*
*gateshead.gov.uk*
*www.gateshead.gov.uk*

## HALTON BOROUGH COUNCIL
Adoption and Fostering Team
Midwood House, Midwood Road
Halton Lea
### RUNCORN
WA8 6BH
*Tel: 01928 704360*
*Email: adoptionandfostering@*
*halton.gov.uk*
*www.halton.gov.uk*

**HARTLEPOOL BOROUGH COUNCIL**
Adoption Team
8–9 Church Street
**HARTLEPOOL**
TS24 7DJ
*Tel: 01429 284596/405589*
*Email: fosterandadopt@hartlepool.*
*gov.uk*
*www.hartlepool.gov.uk*

**HEREFORDSHIRE COUNCIL**
Children's Resource Team
Moor House
Widemarsh Common
**HEREFORD**
HR4 9NA
*Tel: 01432 383240*
*Email: adoption@herefordshire.gov.uk*
*www.herefordshire.gov.uk*

**HULL CITY COUNCIL**
Adoption Services
Children and Young People's Centre
Kenworthy House
104 George Street
**HULL**
HU1 3DT
*Tel: 01482 612800*
*Email: adoption@hullcc.gov.uk*
*www.hullcc.gov.uk*

**ISLE OF MAN GOVERNMENT**
Adoption Service
3 Albany Lane
**DOUGLAS**
Isle of Man
IM2 3NS
*Tel: 01624 625161*
*Email: general@iomas.im*
*www.gov.im*

**KIRKLEES METROPOLITAN COUNCIL**
Family Placement Unit
Westfields, 13 Westfields Road
**MIRFIELD**
WF14 9PW
*Tel: 01924 483707*
*Email: family.placement@*
*kirklees.gov.uk*

*www.kirklees.gov.uk*

**KNOWSLEY METROPOLITAN BOROUGH COUNCIL**
Knowsley Adoption Service
Yorkon Building 2nd Floor
Archway Road
Huyton
**LIVERPOOL**
L36 9YU
*Tel: 0151 443 3958*
*Email: adoption.fostering@knowsley.*
*gov.uk*
*www.knowsley.gov.uk*

**LANCASHIRE COUNTY COUNCIL**
Adoption Recruitment and
Assessment Team
Room B42 County Hall
**PRESTON**
PR1 0LD
*Tel: 0800 028 6349*
*Email: AdoptionRecruitmentand*
*AssessmentTeam@Lancashire.gov.uk.*
*www.lancashire.gov.uk*

**LEEDS CITY COUNCIL**
Fostering and Adoption Service
Merrion House
110 Merrion Centre
8th Floor West
**LEEDS**
LS2 8QB
*Tel:0113 395 2072*
*Email: AdoptionDutyDesk@*
*leeds.gov.uk*
*www.leeds.gov.uk*

**LEICESTER CITY COUNCIL**
Adoption Services East Midlands
provided by Leicester City Council
Eagle House
11 Friar Lane
**LEICESTER**
LE1 5RB
*Tel: 0116 299 5899*
*Email: adoption@leicester.gov.uk*
*www.leicester.gov.uk/adoption*

**LEICESTERSHIRE COUNTY COUNCIL/RUTLAND COUNTY COUNCIL**
Adoption Agency of Leicestershire and Rutland
Room 600, Rutland Building
County Hall
Glenfield
Leicester LE3 8SA
*Tel: 0116 305 3051*
*Email: adoptionteam@leics.gov.uk*
*www.leics.gov.uk*

**LINCOLNSHIRE COUNTY COUNCIL**
Adoption Team
Ground Floor, Orchard House
Orchard Street
**LINCOLN**
LN1 1BA
*Freephone: 0800 093 3099*
*Email: fosteringandadoptionenquiries@
lincolnshire.gov.uk*
*www.lincolnshire.gov.uk*

**CITY OF LIVERPOOL**
Fostering and Adoption Team
Parklands Customer Focus Centre
Conleach Road
Speke
**LIVERPOOL**
L24 0TY
*Tel: 0151 233 3029/3700*
*Email: adoptionserviceduty@
liverpool.gov.uk*
*www.liverpool.gov.uk*

**MANCHESTER CITY COUNCIL**
Family Placement Service
8th Floor Wenlock Way Offices
Wenlock Way
West Gorton
**MANCHESTER**
M12 5DH
*Tel: 0161 274 6287*
*Email: barbara.chambers@manchester.
gov.uk*
*www.manchester.gov.uk*

**MIDDLESBROUGH COUNCIL**
Adoption Team
Middlesbrough Teaching and Learning Centre
Cargo Fleet Lane
**MIDDLESBROUGH**
TS3 8PE
*Tel: 01642 201962/965*
*Email: lynn_woodhouse@middles
borough.gov.uk*
*www.middlesbrough.gov.uk*

**NEWCASTLE CITY COUNCIL**
Children's Services Directorate
Adoption Services
Springfield Centre
Blakelaw
**NEWCASTLE UPON TYNE**
NE5 3HU
*Tel: 0191 211 6777*
*Email: adoption@newcastle.gov.uk*
*www.newcastle.gov.uk*

**NORTHAMPTONSHIRE COUNTY COUNCIL**
Adoption Team
Norborough House
Coverack Close
**NORTHAMPTON**
NN4 8PQ
*Tel: 0300 126 1008*
*Email: a&f@northamptonshire.gov.uk*
*www.northamptonshire.gov.uk*

**NORTH EAST LINCOLNSHIRE COUNCIL**
Adoption Service
Western Technology Site
Cambridge Road
**GRIMSBY**
DN34 5TD
*Tel: 01472 325 545*
*Email: fosteringandadoption@
nelincs.gov.uk*
*www.nelincs.gov.uk*

**NORTH LINCOLNSHIRE COUNCIL**
Adoption Service
Church Square House
30–40 High Street
Scunthorpe
**NORTH LINCOLNSHIRE**
DN15 6NL
*Tel: 01724 297024*
*Email: karen.everatt@northlincs.gov.uk*
*www.northlincs.gov.uk*

**NORTH TYNESIDE COUNCIL**
Children's Services
Adoption Team
Town Hall
High Street East
**WALLSEND**
NE28 7RR
*Tel: 0191 643 2540*
*Email: fosteringandadoption@north
tyneside.gov.uk*
*www.northtyneside.gov.uk/adoption*

**NORTHUMBERLAND COUNTY
COUNCIL**
Family Placement Service
Northumberland County Council
3 Esther Court
**ASHINGTON**
NE63 8AP
*Tel: 01670 534450*
*Email: familysupport@
northumberland.gov.uk*
*www.northumberland.gov.uk*

**NORTH YORKSHIRE COUNTY
COUNCIL**
Adoption Team
Knaresborough Children's Centre
Manor Road
**KNARESBOROUGH**
HG5 0BN
*Tel: 01609 534032*
*Email: adoption@northyorks.gov.uk*
*www.northyorks.gov.uk*

**NOTTINGHAM CITY COUNCIL**
Fostering & Adoption Service
2–6 Isabella Street (3rd Floor)
**NOTTINGHAM**
NG1 6AT
*Tel: 0115 915 1234*
*Email: fa.info@nottinghamcity.gov.uk*
*www.nottinghamcity.gov.uk*

**NOTTINGHAMSHIRE COUNTY
COUNCIL**
Adoption Team Service
Chadburn House
Weighbridge Road
**MANSFIELD**
NG18 1AH
*Tel: 0845 301 2288*
*Email: adoption@nottscc.gov.uk*
*www.nottinghamshire.gov.uk*

**OLDHAM METROPOLITAN
BOROUGH COUNCIL**
Adoption Team
Unit 10 Whitney Court
Southlink Business Park
**OLDHAM**
OL4 1DB
*Tel: 0161 770 6605*
*Email: adoption@oldham.gov.uk*
*www.oldham.gov.uk/adoption*

**REDCAR AND CLEVELAND
BOROUGH COUNCIL**
Adoption Permanency Team
Directorate of Adult & Children's
Services
West Locality Base
Overfields
Daisy Lane
Ormesby
**MIDDLESBROUGH**
TS7 9JF
*Tel: 01642 304500*
*www.redcar-cleveland.gov.uk*

**ROCHDALE METROPOLITAN
BOROUGH COUNCIL**
Adoption Team
Crossfield Mill
Crawford Street
**ROCHDALE**
OL16 5RS
*Tel: 01706 922300*
*Email: adoption@rochdale.gov.uk*
*www.rochdale.gov.uk*

**ROTHERDAM METROPOLITAN
BOROUGH COUNCIL**
Adoption Team
Riverside House
Main Street
**ROTHERHAM**
S60 1AE
*Tel: 01709 254899*
*www.rotherham.gov.uk*

**RUTLAND COUNTY COUNCIL**
See under Leicestershire County
Council

**SALFORD CITY COUNCIL**
Family Placement Team
First Floor
Civic Centre
Chorley Road
Swinton
**MANCHESTER**
M27 5DA
*Tel: 0161 799 1268*
*Email: family.recruitment@salford.
gov.uk*
*www.salford.gov.uk/adoption
andfostering*

**SANDWELL METROPOLITAN
BOROUGH COUNCIL**
Family Placements
PO Box 2374
**OLDBURY**
B69 3DE
*Tel: 0800 358 0899/0845 352 8609*
*Email: adopt_foster@sandwell.gov.uk*
*www.sandwell.gov.uk*

**SEFTON METROPOLITAN BOROUGH
COUNCIL**
Sefton Adoption Service
1st Floor
Merton House
Stanley Road
Bootle
**LIVERPOOL**
L20 3JA
*Tel: 0800 923 2777*
*www.sefton.gov.uk*

**SHEFFIELD CITY COUNCIL**
Adoption Service
Floor 5
Redvers House
Union Street
**SHEFFIELD**
S1 2JQ
*Tel: 0114 273 5010/0114 273 4998*
*Email: adoption@sheffield.gov.uk*
*www.sheffield.gov.uk*

**SHROPSHIRE COUNTY COUNCIL/
TELFORD AND WREKIN COUNCIL**
Joint Adoption Team
Safeguarding
Mount McKinley Building
Shrewsbury Business Park
**SHREWSBURY**
SY2 6FG
*Tel: 01743 250 100*
*Email: ss-adoption@shropshire.gov.uk*
*www.roominyourheartforadoption.co.uk*

**SOLIHULL METROPOLITAN
BOROUGH COUNCIL**
Adoption Team
Education and Children's Services
New House
30 New Road
**SOLIHULL**
B91 3DP
*Tel: 0121 709 0292*
*Email: ssplace@solihull.gov.uk*
*www.solihull.gov.uk*

## SOUTH TYNESIDE METROPOLITAN BOROUGH COUNCIL
Fostering and Adoption Service
16 Barrington Street
**SOUTH SHIELDS**
NE33 1AN
*Tel: 0191 423 8500*
*Email: fostering@southtyneside.gov.uk*
*www.southtyneside.info/fosteringand*
*adoption*

## STAFFORDSHIRE COUNTY COUNCIL
Family Placement Team
Stafford Area Office
Madford Retail Park
Foregate Street
**STAFFORD**
ST16 2PA
*Tel: 0800 169 2061/01785 276875*
*Email: fostering&adoptionbus@*
*staffordshire.gov.uk*
*www.staffordshire.gov.uk*

## ST HELENS METROPOLITAN BOROUGH COUNCIL
St Helens Council, Warrington Council
and Wigan Council
WWiSH Adoption Service
196a Newton Road
Lowton
**WARRINGTON**
WA3 2AQ
*Tel: 01942 487272*
*Email: wwish@wigan.gov.uk*
*www.wigan.gov.uk*

## STOCKPORT METROPOLITAN BOROUGH COUNCIL
Children and Young People's
Directorate
Reddish Green Centre
St Elizabeth's Way
Reddish
**STOCKPORT**
SK5 6BL
*Tel: 0161 442 2055*
*Email: familyplacement@*
*stockport.gov.uk*
*www.stockport.gov.uk*

## STOCKTON-ON-TEES BOROUGH COUNCIL
Child Placement Team
Queensway House (2nd Floor)
West Precinct
Billingham
**STOCKTON-ON-TEES**
TS23 2NL
*Tel: 01642 526218*
*Email: child.placement@*
*stockton.gov.uk*
*www.stockton.gov.uk*

## STOKE-ON-TRENT CITY COUNCIL
Adoption Team
Swann House
Boothen Road
**STOKE-ON-TRENT**
ST4 4SY
*Tel: 01782 235020*
*Email: duty.adoption@stoke.gov.uk*
*www.stoke.gov.uk*

## CITY OF SUNDERLAND
Fostering, Adoption and Permanency
Services
Direct Services
Sandhill Centre
Grindon Lane
**SUNDERLAND**
SR3 4EN
*Tel: 0191 520 5553*
*Email: adopt.foster@sunderland.gov.uk*
*www.sunderland.gov.uk*

## TAMESIDE METROPOLITAN BOROUGH COUNCIL
Children's Social Care
Tameside Adoption Team
Union Street
**HYDE**
SK14 1ND
*Tel: 0161 342 4162/4178*
*www.tameside.gov.uk*

## TELFORD AND WREKIN COUNCIL
See Shropshire County Council

**TRAFFORD METROPOLITAN BOROUGH COUNCIL**
Trafford Adoption Team
Trafford Town Hall
Ground Floor
Talbot Road
Stretford
**MANCHESTER**
M32 0TH
*Tel: 0161 912 3971*
*Email: adoption@trafford.gov.uk*
*www.trafford.gov.uk*

**CITY OF WAKEFIELD METROPOLITAN DISTRICT COUNCIL**
Adoption and Permanence Team
Placement Services, First Floor
Unit 21, Greens Industrial Estate
Caldervale Road
**WAKEFIELD**
WF1 5PH
*Tel: 01924 302160*
*Email: adoption@wakefield.gov.uk*
*www.wakefield.gov.uk*

**WALSALL METROPOLITAN BOROUGH COUNCIL**
Walsall Adoption Service
Pinfold Health Centre
Field Road
Bloxwich
**WALSALL**
WS3 3JJ
*Tel: 0800 923 3706*
*Email: familyplacementsservices@walsall.gov.uk*
*www.walsall.gov.uk*

**WARRINGTON BOROUGH COUNCIL**
See under St Helens Metropolitan Borough Council

**WARWICKSHIRE COUNTY COUNCIL**
Fostering and Adoption Services Team
Saltisford Office Park
Building One
Ansell Way

**WARWICK**
CV34 4UL
*Tel: 01926 746956*
*Email: fosteringadoptiondevelopment team@warwickshire.gov.uk*
*www.warwickshire.gov.uk*

**WIGAN COUNCIL**
See under St Helens Metropolitan Borough Council

**WIRRAL METROPOLITAN BOROUGH COUNCIL**
Adoption Team
Conway Centre
Conway Buildings
118 Conway Street
**BIRKENHEAD**
CH41 6LA
*Tel: 0151 606 2400*
*Email: adoption@wirral.gov.uk*
*www.wirral.gov.uk*

**WOLVERHAMPTON CITY COUNCIL**
Adoption and Fostering Team
Children's Services, Beldray Buildings
66 Mount Pleasant, Bilston
**WOLVERHAMPTON**
WV14 7PR
*Tel: 01902 553818*
*Freephone: 0800 073 0189*
*Email: adoption.team@wolver hampton.gov.uk*
*www.wolverhampton.gov.uk*

**WORCESTERSHIRE COUNTY COUNCIL**
Adoption Service/ Fostering & Kinship Team
PO Box 589
**WORCESTER**
WR4 4AH
*Tel: 0800 633 5442/0800 028 2158*
*Email: cs-adoption&fostering@worcestershire.gov.uk*
*www.worcestershire.gov.uk*

**YORK CITY COUNCIL**
Children's Services
Adoption and Fostering
Hollycroft
Wenlock Terrace
Fulford Road
**YORK**
YO10 4DU
*Tel: 01904 555333*
*Email: adoptionandfostering@*
*york.gov.uk*
*www.york.gov.uk*

# VOLUNTARY AGENCIES

**ACTION FOR CHILDREN ADOPTION
AND FOSTERING MIDLANDS**
Wheatfield Close
Smiths Wood
**BIRMINGHAM**
B36 0QP
*Tel:0121 770 0591*
*www.actionforchildren.org.uk/adoption*

**ACTION FOR CHILDREN ADOPTION
YORKSHIRE**
Granby Road
**HARROGATE**
HG1 4ST
*Tel: 01423 524286*
*Email: vicky.thaxter@actionforchildren.*
*org.uk*
*www.actionforchildren.org.uk/adoption*

**ADOPTION EAST MIDLANDS**
Lacey Court
Charn Wood Road
Shepshed
**LOUGHBOROUGH**
LE12 9QY
*Tel: 01509 600306*
*Email: AdoptEastMids@coram.org.uk*
*www.coram.org.uk*

**ADOPTION FOCUS**
Pinewood Business Park
Coleshill Road

**BIRMINGHAM**
B37 7HG
*Tel: 0845 519 0539*
*Email: info@adoption-focus.org.uk*
*www.adoption-focus.org.uk*

**ADOPTION MATTERS NORTHWEST**
Chester Office
14 Liverpool Road
**CHESTER**
CH2 1AE
*Tel: 01244 390 938*
*Email: info@adoptionmattersnw.org*
*www.adoptionmattersnw.org*

Hale Office
St Peter's House
233 Ashley Road
**HALE**
WA15 9SS
*Tel: 0161 941 7732*
*Email: info@adoptionmattersnw.org*
*www.adoptionmattersnw.org*

Blackburn Office
St Mary's House
Cathedral Close
**BLACKBURN**
BB1 5AA
*Tel: 01254 504740*
*Email: info@adoptionmattersnw.org*
*www.adoptionmattersnw.org*

**BARNARDO'S MIDLANDS NEW
FAMILIES**
Family Placement Services
Trinity House
Trinity Road
**DUDLEY**
DY1 1JB
*Tel: 01384 458 585*
*Email:wnfp@barnados.org.uk*
*www.barnardos.org.uk*

**BARNARDO'S NORTH EAST
FAMILY PLACEMENT**
1 Lumley Court
Drum Industrial Estate
**CHESTER LE STREET**

DH2 1AN
*Tel: 0191 492 9000*
*Email: ne.familyplacement@*
*barnardos.org.uk*
*www.barnardos.org.uk*

**BARNARDO'S YORKSHIRE**
**ADOPTION AND FOSTERING**
Queens House
Queens Road
**BRADFORD**
BD8 7BS
*Tel: 0870 240 8342*
*Email: afby@barnardos.org.uk*
*www.barnardos.org.uk*

**CARITAS CARE (LANCASTER)**
218 Tulketh Road
Ashton on Ribble
**PRESTON**
PR2 1ES
*Tel: 01772 732313*
*Email: info@caritascare.org.uk*
*www.caritascare.org.uk*

**CARITAS DIOCESE OF SALFORD**
**(FORMERLY CATHOLIC CHILDREN'S**
**RESCUE SOCIETY)**
Cathedral Centre
3 Ford Street
**SALFORD**
M3 6DP
*Tel: 0161 817 2250*
*Email: info@caritassalford.org.uk*
*www.caritassalford.org.uk*

**CATHOLIC CARE**
**(DIOCESE OF LEEDS)**
11 North Grange Road
Headingley
**LEEDS**
LS6 2BR
*Tel: 0113 388 5400*
*Email: adoption@catholic-care.org.uk*
*www.catholic-care.org.uk*

**CHILDREN CENTRE FAMILY**
**PLACEMENT SERVICE**
Adoption Team
Bourne House
97 Woodbourne Road
**DOUGLAS**
Isle of Man
IM2 3AW
*Tel: 01624 602912*
*Email: adoption@thechildcentre.org.im*
*www.thechildrenscentre.org.im*

**DFW ADOPTION**
Agriculture House
Stonebridge
**DURHAM**
DH1 3RY
*Tel: 0191 386 3719*
*Email: office@dfw.org.uk*
*www.dfw.org.uk*

**FAITH IN FAMILIES**
**(NOTTINGHAMSHIRE)**
7 Colwick Road
West Bridgford
**NOTTINGHAM**
NG2 5FR
*Tel: 0115 955 8811*
*Email: enquiries@faithinfamilies.org*
*www.faithinfamilies.org*

**FAMILY CARE**
28 Magdala Road
**NOTTINGHAM**
NG3 5DF
*Tel: 0115 960 3010*
*Email: info@familycare-*
*nottingham.org.uk*
*www.familycare-nottingham.org.uk*

**NUGENT CARE ADOPTION SERVICES**
6 Chain Lane
**ST HELENS**
WA11 9RA
*Tel: 0845 270 3531*
*Email: adoption@nugentcare.org*
*www.nugentcare.org*

**YORKSHIRE ADOPTION AGENCY**
Jubilee House
1 Jubilee Road
Wheatley
**DONCASTER**
DN1 2UE
*Tel: 01302 349909*
*Email: info@yorkshireadoption*
*agency.org.uk*
*www.yorkshireadoptionagency.org.uk*

## ENGLAND: SOUTHERN

# BAAF SOUTHERN ENGLAND

Saffron House
6–10 Kirby Street
**LONDON**
EC1N 8TS
*Tel: 020 7421 2670/71*
*Email: southern@baaf.org.uk*
*www.baaf.org.uk*

# LOCAL AUTHORITY AGENCIES

**BARKING AND DAGENHAM, LONDON BOROUGH OF**
Adoption Team
Municipal Offices
127 Ripple Road
**BARKING**
IG11 7PB
*Tel: 020 8227 5854/5949 (Adoption)*
*Email: adoption@lbbd.gov.uk*
*www.lbbd.gov.uk*

**BARNET, LONDON BOROUGH OF**
Adoption Team
North London Business Park
Oakleigh Road South
**LONDON**
N11 1NP
*Tel: 020 8359 5705*
*Email: adoption@barnet.gov.uk*
*www.barnet.gov.uk*

**BATH AND NORTH EAST SOMERSET COUNCIL**
Family Placement Team
Children's Services
Riverside, Temple Street
Keynsham
**BATH**
BS31 1DN
*Tel: 01225 395332*
*Email: fpt_duty@bathnes.gov.uk*
*www.bathnes.gov.uk*

**BEDFORDSHIRE CENTRAL COUNCIL**
Adoption and Family Finding Team
Social Services Department
Unit 5, Franklin Court
Stannard Way
Priory Business Park
**BEDFORD**
MK44 3JZ

*Tel: 0300 300 8181/8090*
*Email: adoptionandfostering@*
*centralbedfordshire.gov.uk*
*www.centralbedfordshire.gov.uk*

**BEXLEY COUNCIL**
Children's Placement Service
London Borough of Bexley
Bexley Civic Offices
Broadway
**BEXLEYHEATH**
DA6 7LB
*Tel: 0800 783 7699*
*Email: adoptionandfostering@*
*bexley.gov.uk*
*www.bexley.gov.uk*

**BOURNEMOUTH BOROUGH COUNCIL**
Adoption Services
Social Services Directorate
North Bournemouth Local Office
27 Slades Farm Road
Ensbury Park
**BOURNEMOUTH**
BH10 4ES
*Tel: 01202 456743*
*Email: adoption@bournemouth.gov.uk*
*www.bournemouth.gov.uk*

**BRACKNELL FOREST BOROUGH COUNCIL**
Family Placement Team
Time Square, Market Street
**BRACKNELL**
RG12 1JD
*Tel: 01344 352020*
*Email: adoption@bracknell-*
*forest.gov.uk*
*www.bracknell-forest.gov.uk*

**BRENT, LONDON BOROUGH OF**
Social Care Placements
Brent Civic Centre
3rd Floor Adoption Team
Engineers Way
**WEMBLEY**
HA9 0FJ

*Tel: 020 8937 4525*
*www.brent.gov.uk*

**BRIGHTON AND HOVE COUNCIL**
Brighton & Hove Fostering and
Adoption Service
Hodshrove Lane
**BRIGHTON**
BN2 4SE
*Tel: 01273 295444*
*Email: fostering.adoption@brighton-*
*hove.gov.uk*
*www.adoptioninbrightonandhove.org.uk*

**BRISTOL CITY COUNCIL**
Social Services Department
Family Placement Team
Avonvale Road
Redfield
**BRISTOL**
BS5 9RH
*Tel: 0117 353 4200*
*Email: fostering.adoption@*
*bristol.gov.uk*
*www.bristol-city.gov.uk*

**BROMLEY, LONDON BOROUGH OF**
Adoption Services Team
Joseph Lancaster Hall
Civic Centre
Rafford Way
**BROMLEY**
BR1 3UH
*Tel: 020 8313 4193*
*Email: adoption@bromley.gov.uk*
*www.bromley.gov.uk*

**BUCKINGHAMSHIRE COUNTY COUNCIL**
Adoption Team
Council Offices
King George V Road
**AMERSHAM**
HP6 5BN
*Tel: 01494 586443*
*Email: adoption@buckscc.gov.uk*
*www.buckscc.gov.uk*

**CAMBRIDGESHIRE COUNTY COUNCIL**
Fostering and Adoption Service
Scott House
5 George Street
**HUNTINGDON**
PE29 3AD
*Tel: 0800 052 0078*
*Email: fanda@cambridgeshire.gov.uk*
*www.cambridgeshire.gov.uk*

**CAMDEN, LONDON BOROUGH OF**
Permanent Placements Team
Phase One, First Floor
Crowndale Centre
218–220 Eversholt Street
**LONDON**
NW1 1BD
*Tel: 020 7974 3082 (Adoption)*
*0800 028 1436 (Freephone)*
*Email: adoption@camden.gov.uk*
*www.camden.gov.uk*

**CORNWALL COUNCIL AND THE COUNCIL OF THE ISLES OF SCILLY ADOPTION AGENCY**
Old County Hall
**TRURO**
TR1 3AY
*Tel: 01872 322200*
*Email: adoption@cornwall.gov.uk*
*www.cornwall.gov.uk*

**CITY OF LONDON**
Department of Communities and
Children's Services
Family and Young People's Services
Guildhall
PO Box 270
**LONDON**
EC2P 2EJ
*Tel: 020 7332 1750*
*Email: social.services@*
*cityoflondon.gov.uk*
*www.cityoflondon.gov.uk*

**CROYDON, LONDON BOROUGH OF**
Adoption Business Support
Croydon Adoption and Permanence
Team
7th Floor Jeanette Wallace House
1 Edridge Road
**CROYDON**
CR0 1FE
*Tel: 020 8726 6000 ext 64025*
*Freephone: 0800 389 0129*
*Email: adoption.enquiries@croydon.*
*gov.uk*
*www.croydon.gov.uk*

**DEVON COUNTY COUNCIL**
Devon Adoption
Follaton House
Plymouth Road
**TOTNES**
TQ9 5RS
*Tel: 0845 155 1013*
*Email: adoption@devon.gov.uk*
*www.devon.gov.uk*

**DORSET COUNTY COUNCIL**
Adoption and Kinship Team
Woodside
Monkton Park
Winterborne Monkton
**DORCHESTER**
DT2 9PS
*Tel: 01305 228200*
*Email: adoption@dorsetcc.gov.uk*
*www.dorsetcc.gov.uk*

**EALING, LONDON BOROUGH OF**
Fostering and Adoption Connections
Perceval House
14–16 Uxbridge Road
Ealing
**LONDON**
W5 2HL
*Tel: 0800 731 6550*
*Email: fosteradopt@ealing.gov.uk*
*www.ealing.gov.uk*

**EAST SUSSEX COUNTY COUNCIL**
County Adoption and Permanence
Team

3rd Floor, St Mark's House
14 Upperton Road
**EASTBOURNE**
BN21 1EP
*Tel: 01323 747154*
*Email: adoption@eastsussex.gov.uk*
*www.eastsussex.gov.uk*

**ENFIELD, LONDON BOROUGH OF**
Social Services Department
Triangle House
305–313 Green Lanes
Palmers Green
**LONDON**
N13 4YB
*Tel: 020 8379 8490*
*Email: adoption@enfield.gov.uk*
*www.enfield.gov.uk/adoption*

**ESSEX COUNTY COUNCIL**
Adoption and Fostering Team
Essex House
200 The Crescent
Colchester Business Park
**COLCHESTER**
CO4 9YQ
*Tel: 0800 801 530*
*Email: adoptionandfostering@*
*essex.gov.uk*
*www.essex.gov.uk*

**GLOUCESTERSHIRE COUNTY**
**COUNCIL**
First Floor
Quayside House
Shirehall
**GLOUCESTER**
GL2 1TP
*Tel: 01242 532597*
*Email: adoption@gloucestershire.*
*gov.uk*
*www.gloucestershire.gov.uk*

**GREENWICH,**
**LONDON BOROUGH OF**
Adoption Team
First Floor The Woolwich Centre
35 Wellington Street

**LONDON**
SE18 6HQ
*Tel: 020 8921 2752*
*Email: adoption@royalgreenwich.*
*gov.uk*
*www.royalgreenwich.gov.uk*

**GUERNSEY, STATES OF**
Fostering and Adoption Services
Swissville Site
Rohais
**ST PETER PORT**
Guernsey
GY1 1FB
*Tel: 01481 713230*
*www.gov.gg*

**HACKNEY, LONDON BOROUGH OF**
Adoption and Fostering
Hackney Service Centre
1 Hillman Street
**LONDON**
E8 1DY
*Tel: 0800 073 0418*
*Email: adoption@hackney.gov.uk*
*www.hackneykids.org.uk*

**HAMMERSMITH AND FULHAM,**
**LONDON BOROUGH OF**
The Royal Borough of Kensington and
Chelsea/City of Westminster Council
Town Hall
4th Floor
King Street
**LONDON**
W6 9JU
*Tel: 0800 781 2332*
*Email: adoption@rbkc.gov.uk*
*www.lbhf.gov.uk*
*www.rbkc.gov.uk*

**HAMPSHIRE COUNTY COUNCIL**
Adoption Services
The Castle
**WINCHESTER**
SO23 8UJ
*Tel: 0845 603 5620*
*Email: adoption.services@hants.gov.uk*
*www.hampshire.gov.uk*

**HARINGEY, LONDON BOROUGH OF**
Adoption Team
40 Cumberland Road
Wood Green
**LONDON**
N22 7SG
*Tel: 020 8489 4610*
*Email: fostering.adoption@haringey.gov.uk*
*www.haringey.gov.uk*

**HARROW COUNCIL**
Family Placement Service
2nd Floor West Wing
Civic Centre
Station Road
**HARROW**
HA1 2XY
*Tel: 0800 064 1000*
*Email: fpuduty@harrow.gov.uk*
*www.harrow.gov.uk*

**HAVERING, LONDON BOROUGH OF**
Adoption Team
Town Hall
Main Road
**ROMFORD**
RM1 3BD
*Tel: 01708 434577*
*Email: adoption@havering.gov.uk*
*www.havering.gov.uk*

**HERTFORDSHIRE COUNTY COUNCIL**
Adoption Team (East and West)
Farnham House
1st Floor
6 Hills Way
**STEVENAGE**
SG1 2FQ
*Tel: 01438 844388*
*Email: FosteringRecruitmentSupport@*
*hertfordshire.gov.uk*
*www.hertsdirect.org*

**HILLINGDON,**
**LONDON BOROUGH OF**
Fostering and Adoption Service
Civic Centre
4S/06 High Street

**UXBRIDGE**
UB8 1UW
*Tel: 0800 783 1298*
*Email: fost-adopt@hillingdon.gov.uk*
*www.hillingdon.gov.uk*

**HOUNSLOW, LONDON**
**BOROUGH OF**
Adoption and Permanence Team
The Civic Centre, Pavillion BF
Lampton Road
**HOUNSLOW**
TW3 4DN
*Tel: 020 8583 4494*
*Email: adoption@hounslow.gov.uk*
*www.hounslow.gov.uk*

**ISLE OF WIGHT COUNCIL**
Adoption Units 1 and 2
Adoption and Fostering Service
Floor 3, County Hall
High Street
**NEWPORT**
Isle of Wight
PO30 1UD
*Tel: 01983 823081/163/434*
*www.iwight.com*

**ISLINGTON, LONDON BOROUGH OF**
Islington Adoption Services
3 Elwood Street
**LONDON**
N5 1EB
*Tel: 0800 0733344/020 7527 4400*
*Email: adoption@islington.gov.uk*
*www.islington.gov.uk/adoption*

**JERSEY, STATES OF**
Fostering and Adoption Jersey
Le Bas Centre
St Saviour's Road
**ST HELIER**
Jersey
JE1 4HR
*Tel: 01534 445273 or 07797811054*
*Email: fosteringandadoption@health.*
*gov.je*
*www.gov.je*

**KENSINGTON AND CHELSEA, ROYAL BOROUGH OF**
See under London Borough of
Hammersmith & Fulham

**KENT COUNTY COUNCIL**
Adoption Service
The Stableblock
Oakwood House
Oakwood Park
**MAIDSTONE**
ME16 8AE
*Tel: 0300 333 5002*
*Email: adoption@kent.gov.uk*
*www.kentadoption.co.uk*

**KINGSTON UPON THAMES, ROYAL BOROUGH OF**
Learning and Children Services
Adoption Team
1st Floor, Guildhall Two
**KINGSTON UPON THAMES**
KT1 1EU
*Tel: 020 8547 6042*
*Email: adoption.duty@rbk.kingston.gov.uk*
*www.kingston.gov.uk*

**LAMBETH, LONDON BOROUGH OF**
Adoption Team
9th Floor, International House
6 Canterbury Crescent
**LONDON**
SW9 7QE
*Tel: 020 7926 8503*
*Email: fosteringandadoption@lambeth.gov.uk*
*www.lambeth.gov.uk*

**LEWISHAM, LONDON BOROUGH OF**
Adoption Service
First Floor
1 Laurence House, Catford Road
**LONDON**
SE6 4RU
*Tel: 0800 587 7392*
*Email: adoption.info@lewisham.gov.uk*
*www.lewisham.gov.uk*

**LUTON COUNCIL**
Social Services Department
Adoption Team
Unity House, 111 Stuart Street
**LUTON**
LU1 5NP
*Tel: 01582 547804*
*Email: adoptions@luton.gov.uk*
*www.luton.gov.uk*

**MEDWAY COUNCIL**
Adoption and Permanence Team
Elaine Centre
Clifton Close
**STROOD**
ME2 2HG
*Tel: 01634 335676*
*Email: adoption@medway.gov.uk*
*www.medway.gov.uk*

**MERTON, LONDON BOROUGH OF**
Adoption and Permanency Team
Merton Civic Centre
London Road
**MORDEN**
SM4 5DX
*Tel: 020 8545 4688*
*Email: adoption@merton.gov.uk*
*www.merton.gov.uk/adoptionandfostering*

**MILTON KEYNES COUNCIL**
Adoption and Fostering
Saxon Court Offices
502 Avebury Boulevard
**MILTON KEYNES**
MK9 3HS
*Tel: 01908 253206*
*Email: AdoptionDuty@milton-keynes.gov.uk*
*www.milton-keynes.gov.uk/adoption-fostering*

**NEWHAM, LONDON BOROUGH OF**
Care Recruitment Team
Newham Dockside
2nd Floor East Wing
1000 Dockside Road
**LONDON**

E16 2QU
*Tel: 0800 013 0393*
*Email: a&frecruitmentteam@newham.*
*gov.uk*
*www.newham.gov.uk*

**NORFOLK COUNTY COUNCIL**
Norfolk Adoption Service
Lakeside 500
Broadland Business Park
Thorpe
**NORWICH**
NR7 0WG
*Tel: 01603 638343*
*Email: adoption@norfolk.gov.uk*
*www.norfolk.gov.uk*

**NORTH SOMERSET DISTRICT**
**COUNCIL**
Adoption Team
Children and Young People's Services
Town Hall
Walliscote Grove Road
**WESTON-SUPER-MARE**
BS23 1UJ
*Tel: 01275 888236*
*Email: adoption@n-somerset.gov.uk*
*www.n-somerset.gov.uk*

**OXFORDSHIRE COUNTY COUNCIL**
Fostering and Adoption
Family Placement Team
21 Between Towns Road
Cowley
**OXFORD**
OX4 3LX
*Tel: 0800 783 5724*
*Email: adoption@oxfordshire.gov.uk*
*www.oxfordshire.gov.uk*

**PETERBOROUGH CITY COUNCIL**
Adoption and Fostering Team
1st Floor Bayard Place
**PETERBOROUGH**
PE1 1AY
*Tel: 01733 317448*
*Email: afuadmin@peterborough.gov.uk*
*www.peterborough.gov.uk*

**PLYMOUTH CITY COUNCIL**
Adoption Team
Midland House
Notte Street
**PLYMOUTH**
PL1 2EJ
*Tel: 01752 306800*
*Email: adoption@plymouth.gov.uk*
*www.plymouth.gov.uk/adoption*

**POOLE BOROUGH COUNCIL**
Adoption and Fostering Team
Children and Young People's Social Care
14A Commercial Road
Parkstone
**POOLE**
BH14 0JW
*Tel: 01202 714711*
*Email: adoption@poole.gov.uk*
*www.poole.gov.uk*

**PORTSMOUTH CITY COUNCIL**
Children, Families and Learning
Adoption and Support Service Centre
Hester Road
**PORTSMOUTH**
PO4 8HB
*Tel: 02392 875294*
*Email: adoptioncentre@portsmouth*
*cc.gov.uk*
*www.portsmouth.gov.uk*

**READING BOROUGH COUNCIL**
Civic Centre
**READING**
RG1 7AE
*Tel: 0118 937 3740*
*Email: adoption@reading.gov.uk*
*www.reading.gov.uk*

**REDBRIDGE,**
**LONDON BOROUGH OF**
Fostering and Adoption Service
Station Road
**BARKINGSIDE**
IG6 1NB
*Tel: 020 8708 7532/7459*
*Email: adoptionteam@redbridge.gov.uk*
*www.redbridgekids.org.uk*

**RICHMOND UPON THAMES, LONDON BOROUGH OF**
Adoption and Permanence Team
Specialist Children's Services
42 York Street
**TWICKENHAM**
TW1 3BW
*Tel: 020 8891 7883*
*Email: adoption@richmond.gov.uk*
*www.richmond.gov.uk*

**SLOUGH BOROUGH COUNCIL**
St Martins Place
Ground Floor
East Wing
51 Bath Road
**SLOUGH**
SL1 3UF
*Tel: 01753 690960/0800 073 0291*
*Email: FamilyPlacementDuty@slough.*
*gov.uk*
*www.slough.gov.uk*

**SOMERSET COUNTY COUNCIL**
Central Adoption Team
Children and Young People's
Department
County Hall B3
**TAUNTON**
TA1 4DY
*Tel: 0800 587 9900*
*Email: childrens@somerset.gov.uk*
*www.adoptioninsomerset.org.uk*

**SOUTH GLOUCESTERSHIRE COUNCIL**
Family Placement Team
PO Box 2082
The Council Offices
Castle Street
Thornbury
**BRISTOL**
BS35 9BQ
*Tel: 01454 868008*
*Email: adoption@southglos.gov.uk*
*www.southglos.gov.uk*

**SOUTHAMPTON CITY COUNCIL**
Civic Centre
**SOUTHAMPTON**
SO14 7LY
*Tel: 023 8083 3004*
*Email: adoption.services@*
*southampton.gov.uk*
*www.southampton.gov.uk*

**SOUTHEND COUNCIL**
Adoption and Fostering Team
The Civic Centre
7th Floor
Victoria Avenue
**SOUTHEND-ON-SEA**
SS2 6ER
*Tel: 01702 212938*
*Email: adoption@southend.gov.uk*
*www.partners-in-adoption.co.uk*

**SOUTHWARK, LONDON BOROUGH OF**
Adoption and Fostering Unit
7 Talfourd Place
Peckham
**LONDON**
SE15 5NW
*Tel: 020 7525 4991/0800 952 0707*
*Email: adoption@southwark.gov.uk*
*www.southwark.gov.uk*

**SUFFOLK COUNTY COUNCIL**
Suffolk Adoption Agency
Endeavour House
Russell Road
**IPSWICH**
IP1 2BX
*Tel: 0800 389 9417*
*Email: adoption@suffolk.gov.uk*
*www.suffolkadoption.com*

**SURREY COUNTY COUNCIL**
Adoption and Permanency Service
Runnymede Centre
Chertsey Road
**ADDLESTONE**
KT15 2EP

*Tel: 0800 096 9626*
*Email: adoption@surreycc.gov.uk*
*www.surreycc.gov.uk*

**SUTTON, LONDON BOROUGH OF**
Adoption and Fostering Team
The Lodge
Honeywood Walk
**CARSHALTON**
SM5 3NX
*Tel: 020 8770 4477*
*Email: suttonadoption@sutton.gov.uk*
*www.sutton.gov.uk*

**SWINDON BOROUGH COUNCIL**
Children's Services Family Placement
Team
Lyndhurst Centre
Lyndhurst Crescent
Park North
**SWINDON**
SN3 2RW
*Tel: 01793 465700*
*Email: familyplacement@*
*swindon.gov.uk*
*www.swindon.gov.uk*

**THURROCK COUNCIL**
Children, Education and Families
Fostering and Adoption Team
PO Box 140
Civic Offices
New Road
**GRAYS**
RM17 6TJ
*Tel: 01375 652617/18*
*Email: fostering.adoption@*
*thurrock.gov.uk*
*www.thurrock.gov.uk*

**TORBAY COUNCIL**
Torbay Adoption Team
Specialist Services
4th Floor North
Tor Hill House c/o Town Hall
Castle Circus
**TORQUAY**
TQ1 3DR

*Tel: 01803 207870*
*Email: adoption.team@torbay.gov.uk*
*www.torbay.gov.uk*

**TOWER HAMLETS,**
**LONDON BOROUGH OF**
Permanency and Adoption Support Team
Mulberry Place
5 Clove Crescent
**LONDON**
E14 2BG
*Tel: 0800 279 9850*
*Email: adoption@towerhamlets.gov.uk*
*www.fosteringandadoption.co.uk*

**WALTHAM FOREST,**
**LONDON BOROUGH OF**
Fostering and Adoption Service
Juniper House
221 Hoe Street
Walthamstow
**LONDON**
E17 9PH
*Tel: 020 8496 1588*
*Email: adoptionassessment@*
*walthamforest.gov.uk*
*www.walthamforest.gov.uk*

**WANDSWORTH,**
**LONDON BOROUGH OF**
Adoption and Fostering Unit
Welbeck House
4th Floor
43–51 Wandsworth High Street
**LONDON**
SW18 2PU
*Tel: 020 8871 6666*
*Email: carerrecruitment@wandsworth.*
*gov.uk*
*www.wandsworth.gov.uk*

**WEST BERKSHIRE COUNCIL**
Family Placement Team
West Street House
West Street
**NEWBURY**
RG14 1BZ

Tel: 01635 503155
Email: jkemp@westberks.gov.uk
www.westberks.gov.uk

**WEST SUSSEX COUNTY COUNCIL**
Adoption Team
County Hall North
Chart Way
**HORSHAM**
RH12 1XH
Tel: 0330 222 7775/01403 229700
Email: fostering.adoption@
westsussex.gov.uk
www.westsussex.gov.uk

**CITY OF WESTMINSTER**
See under London Borough of
Hammersmith & Fulham

**WILTSHIRE COUNTY COUNCIL**
Trowbridge Resource Centre
53 Rutland Crescent
**TROWBRIDGE**
BA14 0NY
Tel: 01225 752198
and
Wiltshire Council Adoption Team
County Hall
Bythesea Road
**TROWBRIDGE**
BA14 8JN
Tel: 0800 169 6321
Email: adoption@wiltshire.gov.uk
www.wiltshire.gov.uk

**WINDSOR AND MAIDENHEAD,
ROYAL BOROUGH OF**
Children's Services Directorate
Fostering, Adoption and Respite
Services
Town Hall
St Ives Road
**MAIDENHEAD**
SL26 1RF
Tel: 01628 683201
Email: adoption-fostering@
rbwm.gov.uk
www.rbwm.gov.uk

**WOKINGHAM DISTRICT COUNCIL**
Children's Services
Placements Service
Brambles Area Office
Budges Gardens
**WOKINGHAM**
RG40 1PX
Tel: 0118 974 6243
Email: familyplacement@wokingham.
gov.uk
www.wokingham.gov.uk

# VOLUNTARY AGENCIES

**ACTION FOR CHILDREN**
Mosaic Adoption and Permanence
Team
12 Hackford Road
**LONDON**
SW9 0QT
Tel: 020 7582 3687
Email: mosaic@actionforchildren.
org.uk
www.actionforchildren.org.uk

**ACTION FOR CHILDREN ADOPTION
SOUTH WEST**
Horner Court
637 Gloucester Road
Horfield
**BRISTOL**
BS7 0BJ
Tel: 0117 958 0158
Email: swaafp@actionforchildren.
org.uk
www.actionforchildren.org.uk

**ADOLESCENT AND CHILDREN'S
TRUST (TACT)**
Head Office
The Courtyard
303 Hither Green Lane
**LONDON**
SE13 6TJ
Tel: 0843 249 7209./020 8695 8142
Email: adoptionduty@tactcare.org.uk
www.tactcare.org.uk

**BARNARDO'S ADOPTION SERVICE**
54 Head Street
**COLCHESTER**
CO1 1PB
*Tel: 01206 562438*
*Email: adoptionservices@barnardos.*
*org.uk*
*www.barnardos.org.uk*

**BARNARDO'S JIGSAW PROJECT**
12 Church Hill
Walthamstow
**LONDON**
E17 3AG
*Tel: 020 8521 0033*
*Email: jigsaw@barnardos.org.uk*
*www.barnardos.org.uk*

**CABRINI CHILDREN'S SOCIETY**
49 Russell Hill Road
**PURLEY**
CR8 2XB
*Tel: 020 8668 2181*
*Email: info@cabrini.org.uk or*
*adoption@cabrini.org.uk*
*www.cabrini.org.uk*

**CABRINI CHILDREN'S SOCIETY**
**BRIGHTON**
Adoption Services
Brighton Junction
1a Isetta Square
35 New England Street
**BRIGHTON**
BN1 4GQ
*Tel: 01273 810280*
*Email: brighton@cabrini.org.uk*
*www.cabrini.org.uk*

**CATHOLIC CHILDREN'S SOCIETY**
**(WESTMINSTER)**
73 St Charles's Square
**LONDON**
W10 6EJ
*Tel: 020 8969 5305*
*Email: info@cathchild.org.uk*
*www.cathchild.org.uk*

**CCS ADOPTION**
162 Pennywell Road
Easton
**BRISTOL**
BS5 0TX
*Tel: 0845 122 0077*
*Email: info@ccsadoption.org*
*www.ccsadoption.org*

**CORAM ADOPT ANGLIA**
9 Petersfield
**CAMBRIDGE**
CB1 1BB
*Tel: 01223 357397*
*Email: anglia@coram-aap.org.uk*
*www.coram.org.uk*

**CORAM FAMILY**
49 Mecklenburgh Square
**LONDON**
WC1N 2QA
*Tel: 020 7520 0300*
*Email: chances@coram.org.uk*
*www.coram.org.uk*

**FAMILIES FOR CHILDREN TRUST**
Southgate Court
Buckfast
**BUCKFASTLEIGH**
TQ11 0EE
*Tel: 01364 645480*
*Email: mail@familiesforchildren.org.uk*
*www.familiesforchildren.org.uk*

**NORWOOD JEWISH ADOPTION**
**SOCIETY**
Broadway House
80–82 The Broadway
**STANMORE**
HA7 4HB
*Tel: 020 8809 8809*
*Email: info@norwood.org.uk*
*www.norwood.org.uk*

**PARENTS AND CHILDREN
TOGETHER (PACT)**
36 Causton Street
Pimlico
**LONDON**
SW18 4AU
*Tel: 020 7592 3923 or 0800 731 1845*
*Email: info@pactcharity.org*
*www.pactcharity.org*

and

7 Southern Court
South Street
**READING**
RG1 4QS
*Tel: 0118 938 7600*
*email: info@pactcharity.org*
*www.pactcharity.org*

**SOLDIERS' SAILORS' AIRMENS'
FAMILIES ASSOCIATION (SSAFA) –
FORCES HELP**
Central Office
4 St Dunstan's Hill
**LONDON**
EC3R 8AD
*Tel: 020 7403 8783*
*Email: info@ssafa.org.uk*
*www.ssafa.org.uk*

**ST FRANCIS' CHILDREN'S SOCIETY**
Collis House
48 Newport Road
Woolstone
**MILTON KEYNES**
MK15 0AA
*Tel: 01908 572700*
*Email: enquiries@sfcs.org.uk*
*www.sfcs.org.uk*

**TACT CARE**
303 Hither Green Lane
**LONDON**
SE13 6TJ
*Tel: 0843 249 7209*
*Email: adoptionduty@tactcare.org.uk*
*www.tactcare.org.uk*

## CYMRU

## BAAF CYMRU

7 Cleeve House
Lambourne Crescent
**CARDIFF**
CF14 5GP
*Tel: 029 2076 1155*
*Email: cardiff@baaf.org.uk*


and at


W2
Morfa Clwyd Business Centre
84 Marsh Road
**RHYL**
LL18 2AF
*Tel: 01745 336336*
*Email: rhyl@baaf.org.uk*

## North Wales Adoption Service

Room 7
Crown Buildings
31 Chester Street
**WREXHAM**
LL13 8BG
*Tel: 01978 295311*
*Email: adoption@wrexham.gov.uk*

## South Wales Adoption Consortium

Address as BAAF Cardiff
*Tel: 029 2076 4849*
*Email: swaac@baaf.org.uk*

---

# LOCAL AUTHORITY AGENCIES

NOTE:  Starred councils (*) in Wales are now part of the North Wales Adoption Service – Central enquiries:
*Tel: 0800 085 0774*
*Email: info@northwalesadoption.co.uk*
*www.northwalesadoption.co.uk*

### ANGLESEY COUNTY COUNCIL, ISLE OF

Children Services
Council Building
**LLANGEFNI**
Anglesey
LL77 7TW
*Tel: 01248 752722/752733*
*Email: csdss@anglesey.gov.uk*
*www.anglesey.gov.uk*

### BLAENAU GWENT COUNTY BOROUGH COUNCIL

South East Wales Adoption Service
Monmouthshire County Council/
Torfaen County Council

Ebbw Vale Social Services
7 Bridge Street
**EBBW VALE**
NP23 6EY
*Tel: 01495 355766*
*Email: adoption@blaenau-*
*gwent.gov.uk*
*www.blaenau-gwent.gov.uk*

**BRIDGEND COUNTY BOROUGH COUNCIL**
Personal Services Directorate
Adoption Team
Sunnyside
**BRIDGEND**
CF31 4AR
*Tel: 01656 815180*
*Email: adoption@bridgend.gov.uk*
*www.bridgend.gov.uk*

**CAERPHILLY COUNTY BOROUGH COUNCIL**
Adoption Team
Penallta House
Tredomen Park
Ystrad Mynach
**HENGOED**
CF82 7PG
*Tel: 01443 864527*
*Email: adoption@caerphilly.gov.uk*
*www.caerphilly.gov.uk*

**CARDIFF COUNCIL**
Children's Services
Fostering/Adoption Service
St Mellons Family Centre
112 Heol Maes Eirwg
St Mellons
**CARDIFF**
CF3 0JZ
*Tel: 029 2087 3797*
*Email: adoptionadmin@cardiff.gov.uk*
*www.cardiff.gov.uk*

**CARMARTHENSHIRE COUNTY COUNCIL**
West Wales Adoption Team
Building 1
St Davids Park
**CARMARTHEN**
SA31 3HB
*Tel: 01267 246970*
*Email: adoptionenquiries@carmarthen*
*shire.gov.uk*
*www.carmarthenshire.gov.uk*

**CEREDIGION COUNTY COUNCIL**
West Wales Adoption Service
Minaeron
Rhiw Goch
**ABERAERON**
SA46 0DY
*Tel: 01545 574077/4078*
*Email: contact-socservs@ceredigion.*
*gov.uk*
*www.ceredigion.gov.uk*

**\*CONWY COUNTY BOROUGH COUNCIL**
Denbighshire County Council/Flintshire
County Council/Gwynedd
Council/Wrexham Council
North Wales Adoption Service
Crown Buildings
31 Chester Street
**WREXHAM**
LL13 8BG
*Tel: 01978 295311/0800 085 0774*
*www.northwalesadoption.gov.uk*

**\*DENBIGHSHIRE COUNTY COUNCIL**
See under Conwy County Borough
Council

**\*FLINTSHIRE COUNTY COUNCIL**
See under Conwy County Borough
Council

**\*GWYNEDD COUNCIL**
See under Conwy County Borough
Council

**ISLE OF ANGLESEY COUNTY COUNCIL**
See Anglesey County Council

**MERTHYR TYDFIL COUNTY BOROUGH COUNCIL**
The Fostering & Adoption Team
Unit 5
Triangle Business Park
Pentrebach
**MERTHYR TYDFIL**
CF48 4TQ
*Tel: 0800 678 3798*
*Email: foster.adopt@merthyr.gov.uk*

**MONMOUTHSHIRE COUNTY COUNCIL**
See under Blaenau Gwent County Borough

**NEATH PORT TALBOT COUNTY BOROUGH COUNCIL**
The Adoption Team
Social Services, Health and Housing
Neath Civic Centre
**NEATH**
SA11 3QZ
*Tel: 01639 686854*
*Email: adoption@npt.gov.uk*
*www.npt.gov.uk*

**NEWPORT CITY COUNCIL**
Adoption & Permanence Team
Newport City Council
Civic Centre
Godfrey Road
**NEWPORT**
NP20 4UR
*Telephone: 01633 656656*
*Email: adoption@newport.gov.uk*
*www.newport.gov.uk*

**PEMBROKESHIRE COUNTY COUNCIL**
West Wales Adoption Service
The Elms
Golden Hill Road
**PEMBROKE**

SA71 4QB
*Tel: 01437 774650/01646 683747*
*Email: adoptionenquiries@ carmarthenshire.gov.uk*
*www.pembrokeshire.gov.uk*

**POWYS COUNTY COUNCIL**
Adoption Team (North)
The Park
**NEWTON**
SY16 2PL
*Tel: 01686 617520*
and

Adoption Team (South)
Neuadd Brycheiniog
Cambrian Way
**BRECON**
LD3 7HR
*Tel: 01874 614030*
*Email: adoption@powys.gov.uk*
*www.powys.gov.uk*

**RHONDDA CYNON TAF COUNTY BOROUGH COUNCIL**
Adoption Service
Rhondda-Cynon-Taff CBC
Ty Pennant
Catherine Street
**PONTYPRIDD**
CF37 2TB
*Tel: 01443 490460*
*Email: angela.harris@rctcbc.gov.uk*
*www.rctcbc.gov.uk*

**SWANSEA, CITY AND COUNTY OF**
Adoption Section
Family Placement Team
Cockett House
Cockett Road
Cockett
**SWANSEA**
SA2 0FJ
*Tel: 01792 522900*
*Email: adopt.swansea@swansea.gov.uk*
*www.swansea.gov.uk*

**TORFAEN COUNTY BOROUGH COUNCIL**
See under Blaenau Gwent County Council

**VALE OF GLAMORGAN COUNCIL**
Placements and Permanency
Haydock House
1 Holton Road
**BARRY**
CF63 4HA
*Tel: 01446 729600*
*Email: adoption@*
*valeofglamorgan.gov.uk*
*www.valeofglamorgan.gov.uk*

**\*WREXHAM COUNTY BOROUGH COUNCIL**
See under Conwy County Borough Council

SA11 1LF
*Tel: 01639 620771*
*www.barnardos.org.uk*

**ST DAVID'S CHILDREN'S SOCIETY**
28 Park Place
**CARDIFF**
CF10 3BA
*Tel: 029 2066 7007*
*Email: info@stdavidsscs.org*
*www.adoptionwales.org*

# VOLUNTARY AGENCIES

**ADOLESCENT AND CHILDREN'S TRUST (TACT)**
TACT Cymru
20 Victoria Gardens
**NEATH**
SA11 3BH
*Tel: 01639 622320/0800 169 6895*
*Email: cymru@tactcare.org.uk*
*www.tactcare.org.uk*

**BARNARDO'S**
Barnardo's Cymru
Trident Court
East Moors Road
**CARDIFF**
CF24 5TD
*Tel: 029 2049 3387*
and

South West Wales Office
Barnardo's Cymru
19–20 London Road
**NEATH**

## SCOTLAND

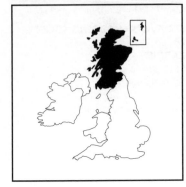

## BAAF SCOTLAND
113 Rose Street
**EDINBURGH**
EH2 3DT
*Tel: 0131 226 9270*
*Email: scotland@baaf.org.uk*

## West of Scotland Family Placement Consortium
Address as above
*Tel: 0131 226 9272*
*Email: west.scotland@*
*baaf.org.uk*

## North East of Scotland Family Placement Consortium
Address as above
*Tel: 0131 226 9271*
*Email: north.scotland@*
*baaf.org.uk*

# LOCAL AUTHORITY AGENCIES

**ABERDEEN CITY COUNCIL**
Neighbourhood Services Social Work
Adoption and Fostering Team
77/79 King Street
**ABERDEEN**
AB24 5AB
*Tel: 01224 793830*
*Email: adoptfost@aberdeencity.gov.uk*
*www.aberdeencity.gov.uk*

**ABERDEENSHIRE COUNCIL**
Social Work Department
Carlton House
Arduthie Road
**STONEHAVEN**
AB39 2DL
*Tel: 01467 625555*
*Email: adoption@aberdeenshire.gov.uk*
*www.aberdeenshire.gov.uk*

**ANGUS COUNCIL**
Family Placement Team
Academy Lane
**ARBROATH**
DD11 1EJ
*Tel: 01241 435078*
*Email: fosteringandadoption@*
*angus.gov.uk*
*www.angus.gov.uk*

**ARGYLL AND BUTE COUNCIL**
Family Placement Team
29 Lomond Street
Lomond House
**HELENSBOROUGH**
G84 7PW
*Tel: 01546 605522*
*Email: janice.frank@argyll-bute.gov.uk*
*www.argyll-bute.gov.uk*

**CLACKMANNANSHIRE COUNCIL**
Child Care Services
Lime Tree House
North Castle Street

**ALLOA**
FK10 1EX
*Tel: 01259 225000*
*Email: childcare@clacks.gov.uk*
*www.clacksweb.org.uk*

**COMHAIRLE NAN EILEAN SIAR
(WESTERN ISLES COUNCIL)**
Social Work Department
Council Offices
Rathad Shanndabhaig (Sandwick Road)
**STEORNABHAGH (STORNOWAY)**
Isle of Lewis
HS1 2BW
*Tel: 0845 600 7090*
*Email: enquiries@cne-siar.gov.uk*
*www.cne-siar.gov.uk*

**DUMFRIES AND GALLOWAY
COUNCIL**
Fostering and Adoption Team
122–124 Irish Street
**DUMFRIES**
DG1 2AW
*Tel: 01387 273600*
*Email: sandra.richie@dumgal.gov.uk*
*www.dumgal.gov.uk*

**DUNDEE CITY COUNCIL**
Dudhope Castle
Barrack Road
**DUNDEE**
DD3 6HF
*Tel: 01382 436060*
*www.dundeecity.gov.uk*

**EAST AYRSHIRE COUNCIL**
Fostering and Adoption Team
The Johnnie Walker Bond
15 Strand Street
**KILMARNOCK**
KA1 1HU
*Tel: 01563 576905/0800 434 6633*
*Email: fostering&adoption@
east-ayrshire.gov.uk*
*www.east-ayrshire.gov.uk*

**EAST DUNBARTONSHIRE COUNCIL**
Social Work
Adoption and Fostering
Southbank House
Strathkelvin Place
**KIRKINTILLOCH**
G66 1XQ
*Tel: 0141 777 3003*
*Email: familybasedcare@east
dunbarton.gov.uk*
*www.eastdunbarton.gov.uk*

**EAST LOTHIAN COUNCIL**
The Family Placement Team
Randall House
Macmerry Business Park
**TRANENT**
EH33 1RW
*Tel: 01620 827643*
*Email: familyplacement@eastlothian.
gov.uk*
*www.eastlothian.gov.uk*

**EAST RENFREWSHIRE COUNCIL**
Fostering and Adoption
Lygates House, 224–226 Ayr Road
Newton Mearns
**GLASGOW**
G77 6FR
*Tel: 0141 577 3367*
*www.eastrenfrewshire.gov.uk*

**CITY OF EDINBURGH COUNCIL**
Family Based Care Recruitment Team
Springwell House
1 Gorgie Road
**EDINBURGH**
EH11 2LA
*Tel: 0800 174833*
*Email: adoptchildren@edinburgh.
gov.uk*
*www.edinburgh.gov.uk*

**FALKIRK COUNCIL**
Social Work Services
Adoption and Fostering Team
Grangemouth Social Work Office
Oxgang Road

**GRANGEMOUTH**
FK3 9EF
*Tel: 01324 504343*
*Email:fosteringandadoptionteam@*
*falkirk.gov.uk*
*www.falkirk.gov.uk*

**FIFE COUNCIL**
Family Placement Team
New City House
1 Edgar Street
**DUNFERMLINE**
KY12 7EP
*Tel: 0345 155 0000*
*www.fife.gov.uk*

**GLASGOW CITY COUNCIL**
Families for Children
136 Stanley Street
**GLASGOW**
G41 1JH
*Tel: 0141 420 5555/0845 270 0609*
*Email: families.children@sw.glasgow.*
*gov.uk*
*www.glasgow.gov.uk*

**HIGHLAND COUNCIL**
Family Resource Centre
Limetree Avenue
**INVERNESS**
IV3 5RH
*Tel: 01463 703431*
*Email: fostering@highland.gov.uk*
*www.highland.gov.uk*

**INVERCLYDE COUNCIL**
Children and Families Section
Ravenscraig Hospital
Inverkip Road
**GREENOCK**
PA16 9HA
*Tel: 01475 714038/39*
*Email: fosteringandadoption@*
*inverclyde.gov.uk*
*www.inverclyde.gov.uk*

**MIDLOTHIAN COUNCIL**
Family Placement Team
Adoption and Fostering

Lawfield Primary School
26 Lawfield Road
Mayfield
**DALKEITH**
EH22 5BB
*Tel: 0131 270 5678*
*Email: family.placement@midlothian.*
*gov.uk*
*www.midlothian.gov.uk*

**MORAY COUNCIL**
Fostering and Adoption Team
6 Moss Street
**ELGIN**
IV30 1LU
*Tel: 01343 563568*
*Email: foster.adopt@moray.org.uk*
*www.moray.org*

**NORTH AYRSHIRE COUNCIL**
Family Placement Team
Social Services
47 West Road
**IRVINE**
KA12 8RE
*Tel: 01294 311505*
*Email: adfos-enquiry@north-*
*ayrshire.gov.uk*
*www.north-ayrshire.gov.uk*

**NORTH LANARKSHIRE COUNCIL**
Fostering and Adoption Team
Children's Carers' Centre
7 Mitchell Street
**AIRDRIE**
ML6 0EB
*Tel: 0800 073 1566*
*Email: northrecservices@*
*northlan.gov.uk*
*www.northlan.gov.uk*

**ORKNEY ISLANDS COUNCIL**
Children and Families Team
Council Offices
School Place
**KIRKWELL**
KW15 1NY
*Tel: 01856 873535*

*Email: social.services@orkney.gov.uk*
*www.orkney.gov.uk*

**PERTH AND KINROSS COUNCIL**
Permanence Team
Colonsay Resource Centre
**PERTH**
PH1 3TU
*Tel: 01738 783450*
*Email: ecsfosteringandadoption@*
*pkc.gov.uk*
*www.pkc.gov.uk*

**RENFREWSHIRE COUNCIL**
Renfrewshire Fostering and Adoption
Services
Paisley Office
Abbey House
8 Seedhill Road
**PAISLEY**
PA1 1JT
*Tel: 0300 300 1199*
*Email: childrenandfamilies.sw@*
*renfrewshire.gov.uk*
*www.renfrewshire.gov.uk*

**SCOTTISH BORDERS COUNCIL**
Adoption Fostering and Family
Placement
Paton St
**GALASHIELS**
TD1 3DL
*Tel: 01896 662799*
*www.scotborders.gov.uk*

**SHETLAND ISLANDS COUNCIL**
Family Placement Team
Hayfield House
Hayfield Lane
**LERWICK**
Shetland
ZE1 0QD
*Tel: 01595 744400*
*Email: fosteringandadoptionteam@*
*shetland.gov.uk*
*www.shetland.gov.uk*

**SOUTH AYRSHIRE COUNCIL**
Family Placement and Adoption Team
Whitlets Area Centre
181 Whitlets Road
**AYR**
KA8 0JQ
*Tel: 01292 267675*
*Email: fostering@south-ayrshire.gov.uk*
*www.south-ayrshire.gov.uk*

**SOUTH LANARKSHIRE COUNCIL**
Social Work Department
Adoption and Fostering
4th Floor
Brandongate
1 Leachlee Road
**HAMILTON**
ML3 0XB
*Tel: 01698 454895*
*Email: familyplacement@south*
*lanarkshire.gov.uk*
*www.southlanarkshire.gov.uk*

**STIRLING COUNCIL**
Adoption
Municipal Buildings
8–10 Corn Exchange Road
**STIRLING**
FK8 2HU
*Tel: 01786 471177*
*Email: adoption-fostering@*
*stirling.gov.uk*
*www.stirling.gov.uk*

**WEST DUNBARTONSHIRE COUNCIL**
Adoption and Fostering Team
West Dunbartonshire
CHCP Childcare Section
1st Floor
Bridge Street
**DUMBARTON**
G82 1NT
*Tel: 01389 772165/772166*
*Email: fostering@west-dunbarton.*
*gov.uk*
*www.west_dunbarton.gov.uk*

**WEST LOTHIAN COUNCIL**
Family Placement Team
189a West Main Street
**BROXBURN**
EH52 5LH
*Tel: 01506 775677*
*Email: fostercare@westlothian.gov.uk*
*www.westlothian.gov.uk*

**WESTERN ISLES COUNCIL**
See Comhairle Nan Eilean Siar

**SCOTTISH ADOPTION ASSOCIATION**
161 Constitution Street
Leith
**EDINBURGH**
EH6 7AD
*Tel: 0131 553 5060*
*Email: info@scottishadoption.org*
*www.scottishadoption.org*

# VOLUNTARY AGENCIES

**BARNARDO'S FAMILY PLACEMENT
SERVICES**
6 Torphichen Street
**EDINBURGH**
EH3 8JQ
*Tel: 0131 228 4121*
*www.barnardos.org.uk*

**BIRTHLINK**
21 Castle Street
**EDINBURGH**
EH2 3DN
*Tel: 0131 225 6441*
*Email: mail@birthlink.org.uk*
*www.birthlink.org.uk*

**ST ANDREW'S CHILDREN'S SOCIETY**
7 John's Place
Leith
**EDINBURGH**
EH6 7EL
*Tel: 0131 454 3370*
*Email: info@standrews-children.org.uk*
*www.standrews-children.org.uk*

**ST MARGARET'S CHILDREN AND
FAMILY CARE SOCIETY**
274 Bath Street
**GLASGOW**
G2 4JR
*Tel: 0141 332 8371*
*Email: info@stmargarets
adoption.org.uk*
*www.stmargarets-cafcs.org.uk*

## NORTHERN IRELAND

### BAAF NORTHERN IRELAND
Botanic House
1–5 Botanic Avenue
**BELFAST**
BT7 1JG
*Tel: 028 9031 5494*
*Email: northernireland@*
*baaf.org.uk*

---

In Northern Ireland, you can contact
either the Regional Adoption and
Fostering Service, or your local Health
and Social Care Trust.

### REGIONAL ADOPTION AND FOSTERING SERVICE
Nore Villa
Knockbracken Healthcare Park
Saintfield Road
**BELFAST**
BT8 8BH
*Tel: 0800 072 0137/028 4504 6706*
*Email: info@adoptionandfostering.*
*hscni.net*
*www.adoptionandfostering.hscni.net*

# HEALTH AND SOCIAL CARE TRUSTS

### BELFAST HEALTH AND SOCIAL CARE TRUST
Adoption Team
33 Wellington Park
**BELFAST**
BT9 6DL
*Tel: 028 9504 0350*
*www.belfasttrust.hscni.net*

### NORTHERN HEALTH AND SOCIAL CARE TRUST
Adoption Support Team
Unit 3 Springfarm Industrial Estate
Ballymena Road
**ANTRIM**
BT41 4NT
*Tel: 028 9448 8285*
*www.northerntrust.hscni.net*

### SOUTH EASTERN HEALTH AND SOCIAL CARE TRUST
Adoption and Permanency Team
Warren Children's Centre
61 Woodland Park
**LISBURN**
BT28 1LQ
*Tel: 028 9260 7528*
*www.setrust.hscni.net*

and

Adoption Service
57/58 Dunlop Units
4 Balloo Drive
**BANGOR**
BT19 7QY
*Tel: 028 9127 0672*
*www.setrust.hscni.net*

### SOUTHERN HEALTH AND SOCIAL CARE TRUST
Family Placement Service
Drumalane House
Drumalane Road

**NEWRY**
BT35 8AP
*Tel: 028 3083 2693*
*www.southerntrust.hscni.net*

and

Family Placement Service
Drumglass Lodge
20 Coalisland Road
**DUNGANNON**
BT71 6LA
*Tel: 028 8775 2033*
*www.southerntrust.hscni.net*

**WESTERN HEALTH AND SOCIAL
CARE TRUST**
Rossdowney House
Glendermott Road
**DERRY**
BT47 6BS
*Tel: 028 7131 4226*
*www.westerntrust.hscni.net*

and

Adoption and Permanency
Tyrone and Fermanagh Hospital
Hospital Road
**OMAGH**
BT79 7EQ
*Tel: 028 8283 5114*
*www.westerntrust.hscni.net*

# VOLUNTARY AGENCIES

**ADOPTION ROUTES**
Unit 2
18 Heron Road
**BELFAST**
BT3 9LE
*Tel: 028 9082 8830*
*Email: info@adoptionroutes.co.uk*
*www.adoptionroutes.co.uk*

**FAMILY CARE SOCIETY (NORTHERN
IRELAND)**
511 Ormeau Road
**BELFAST**
BT7 3GS
*Tel: 028 9069 1133*
*www.familycaresociety.co.uk*

# Useful organisations

## British Association for Adoption & Fostering (BAAF) www.baaf.org.uk

BAAF is the leading UK-wide organisation for all those working in the adoption, fostering and childcare fields. BAAF's work includes giving advice and information to members of the public on aspects of adoption, fostering and childcare issues; publishing a wide range of books, training packs and leaflets as well as a quarterly journal on adoption, fostering and childcare issues; providing training and consultancy services to social workers and other professionals to help them improve the quality of medical, legal and social work services to children and families; giving evidence to government committees on subjects concerning children and families; responding to consultative documents on changes in legislation and regulations affecting children in or at risk of coming into care; and helping to find new families for children through Be My Parent.

Almost all local authority and voluntary adoption agencies are members of BAAF. You can join BAAF as an individual member; contact the Membership Officer on 020 7421 2635 or visit www.baaf.org.uk for details of benefits and fees. BAAF is a registered charity.

## Be My Parent

Every month, between 200 and 250 children waiting for new permanent families are featured in *Be My Parent*, the UK-wide family-finding newspaper published by BAAF, and between 300 and nearly 500 on BMP online, the accompanying website. Subscribers include approved adopters, those waiting to be approved and those who have only just begun to think about adopting or permanently fostering. Children of all ages and with a wide range of needs are featured, and therefore *Be My Parent* seeks as wide a readership as possible. Many hundreds of families (married couples and single people) have adopted after first having seen their child's photograph and read their profile in *Be My Parent.* To subscribe and have the newspaper sent directly to you, just telephone the number below. If you see children in *Be My Parent* whom you would like to become part of your family, one phone call to our staff will begin the process that could lead to you being approved to adopt that child.

**Be My Parent** is at

**BAAF**
Saffron House
6–10 Kirby Street
London EC1N 8TS
*Tel: 020 7421 2666/2663*
*Email: bmp@baaf.org.uk*
*www.bemyparent.org.uk*

## West of Scotland and North East of Scotland Family Placement Consortia

These two consortia facilitate the placement of children across local authority boundaries in their particular areas in Scotland. For contact details of the consortia, see p120.

## South Wales Adoption Agencies Consortium (SWAAC)

Nine local authorities and two voluntary adoption agencies co-operate to link children with waiting adopters. BAAF Cymru supervises the co-ordinator and administrator on behalf of the SWAAC management group.

# BAAF offices

## Head Office
Saffron House
6–10 Kirby Street
London EC1N 8TS
*Tel: 020 7421 2600*
*Fax: 020 7421 2601*
*Email: mail@baaf.org.uk*

## BAAF Scotland
113 Rose Street
Edinburgh EH2 3DT
*Tel: 0131 226 9270*
*Fax: 0131 226 2503*
*Email: scotland@baaf.org.uk*

## BAAF Cymru
7 Cleeve House
Lambourne Crescent
Cardiff CF14 5GP
*Tel: 029 2076 1155*
*Fax: 029 2074 7934*
*Email: cardiff@baaf.org.uk*

## BAAF Northern Ireland
Botanic House
1–5 Botanic Avenue
Belfast BT7 1JG
*Tel: 028 9031 5494*
*Fax: 028 9031 4516*
*Email: northernireland@baaf.org.uk*

## BAAF Southern England
Address as Head Office
*Tel: 020 7421 2671*
*Fax: 020 7421 2669*
*Email: southern@baaf.org.uk*

## BAAF Northern England
Unit 4
Pavilion Business Park
Royds Hall Road
Leeds LS12 6AJ
*Tel: 0113 289 1101*
*Email: leeds@baaf.org.uk*

# Adoption Register for England and Wales

The Adoption Register is a database of waiting approved adopters and children for whom adoption is the plan. It has been fully operational since April 2002 and has been run by BAAF on behalf of the Department for Education since December 2004. Its purpose is to increase the opportunities of finding a family for children waiting for adoption. Only adoption agencies in England and Wales can refer adopters and children to the Register.

The Register has two main elements. Firstly, there is the computer database which stores the details of children waiting and families approved. Secondly, there is a team of experienced database operators and social workers who look into the information that is held and suggest potential matches between children and prospective adopters.

Local authority adoption agencies will be expected to refer children for whom adoption is the plan three months after this decision has been made, if a local match has not been identified. They must also refer prospective adopters three months after their approval, if they have not already had a child matched with them. Although they are not obliged to do so most voluntary adoption agencies also choose to refer adopters they have approved. All families must give their consent before they can be referred by their agency and can also refer themselves to the Register three months after approval.

Prospective adopters can contact Register staff directly for general advice, and to check that they are on referral and their details are correct. They will be informed if their details have or have not been sent out as a possible link, but will be advised to contact their social worker for further details about the child or children involved.

**Adoption Register for England and Wales**
Unit 4, Pavilion Business Park
Royds Hall Road, Wortley
Leeds LS12 6AJ
*Adopters' Helpline: 0845 450 3931*

*Email: mail@adoptionregister.org.uk*
*www.adoptionregister.org.uk*

## Adoption Regional Information System for Northern Ireland (ARIS)

ARIS has been operational since the summer of 2010. It is run by BAAF on behalf of DHSSPS (NI). It operates in a similar way to the Adoption Register for England and Wales.

**ARIS NI**
BAAF Northern Ireland
Botanic House
1–5 Botanic Avenue
Belfast BT7 1JG
*Tel: 028 9031 9070*
*Email: aris@baaf.org.uk*
*www.ni-aris.org.uk*

## Scotland's Adoption Register

Scotland's Adoption Register was launched in 2011. It is run by BAAF on behalf of the Scottish Government. It operates in a similar way to the Adoption Register for England and Wales.

**Scotland's Adoption Register**
113 Rose Street
Edinburgh EH2 3DT
*Tel: 0131 226 9279*
*Email: sar@scotlandsadoptionregister.org.uk*
*www.scotlandsadoptionregister.org.uk*

# Organisations for parents

## Adoption UK

Adoption UK is a parent-to-parent network of over 3,500 established and potential adoptive families. It welcomes enquiries from prospective adopters; offers local support groups across the UK; publishes a range of useful leaflets and *Adoption Today* – a monthly magazine written by and for adopters, which also features children waiting for adoption. Visit their website for membership details.

**Adoption UK**
Linden House
55 The Green
South Bar Street
Banbury  OX16 9AB
*Tel: 01295 752240*
*Helpline: 0844 848 7900*
*Email: admin@adoptionuk.org.uk*
*www.adoptionuk.org.uk.*

## First4Adoption

A dedicated information service for people interested in adopting a child from England.
Information line: 10am–6pm Monday–Friday
*Tel: 0300 222 0022*
*Email: helpdesk@first4adoption.org.uk*
*www.first4adoption.org.uk*

## OASIS (Overseas Adoption Support and Information Service)

A UK-based voluntary support group for people who wish to adopt, or have already adopted, children from overseas.

**OASIS**
*www.adoptionoverseas.org*

## Contact a Family

Contact a Family is a charity for any parent or professional involved with or caring for a child with disabilities. Through a network of mutual support and self-help groups, Contact a Family brings together families whose children have disabilities, and offers advice to parents who wish to start a support group.

**Contact a Family**
209–211 City Road
London EC1V 1JN
*Tel: 0207 608 8700*
*Helpline: 0808 808 3555*
*Textphone: 0808 808 3556*
*Email: info@cafamily.org.uk*
*www.cafamily.org.uk*

# Post and after adoption centres

There are many well established adoption support services that provide a service for adoptive families, adopted people and birth parents whose children were adopted. Many offer advice and counselling, in person, but also on the telephone or by correspondence, for individuals and families. Some also organise adoption-related events and enable people to meet in common interest groups.

## Post-Adoption Centre
5 Torriano Mews, Torriano Avenue
London NW5 2RZ
*Tel: 020 7284 0555*
*Email: advice@postadoptioncentre.org.uk*
*www.pac.org.uk*

## After Adoption
5 Blantyre Street
Manchester
M15 4JJ
*Tel: 0161 839 4932*
*Action line: 0800 056 8578*
*Email: information@afteradoption.org.uk*
*www.afteradoption.org.uk*
After Adoption has a number of regional offices around the UK

## After Adoption Midlands
1st Floor
New Oxford House
16 Waterloo Street
Birmingham
B2 5UG
*Tel: 0121 666 6014*

## After Adoption Yorkshire
Hollyshaw House
2 Hollyshaw Lane
Leeds
Yorkshire
LS15 7BD
*Tel: 0113 230 2100*
*Email: info@aay.org.uk*
*www.afteradoptionyorkshire.org.uk*

## Birthlink

21 Castle Street
Edinburgh EH2 3DN
*Tel: 0131 225 6441*

*Email: mail@birthlink.org.uk*
*www.birthlink.org.uk*

**Barnardo's Scottish Adoption Advice Service**
Suite 5/3, Skypark SPS
45 Finnieston Street
Glasgow G3 8JU
*Tel: 0141 248 7530*
*Email: adoptscot@barnardos.org.uk*
*www.barnardos.org.uk*

**Adoption Routes**
**(formerly The Church of Ireland Adoption Society)**
Ground Floor, Unit 2
18 Heron Road
Belfast BT3 9LE
*Tel: 028 9073 6080*
*Email: info@adoptionroutes.co.uk*
*www.adoptionroutes.co.uk*

Local authorities may also provide help and support. In Scotland, they have a duty to help adoptive families, adopted children and birth families. They sometimes use voluntary agencies for this.

# Fostering

**Fostering Network**
87 Blackfriars Road
London SE1 8HA
*Tel: 020 7620 6400*
*Email: info@fostering.net*
*www.fostering.net*

**Fostering Network (Scotland)**
Ingram House, 2nd Floor
227 Ingram Street
Glasgow G11DA

*Tel: 0141 204 1400*
*Email: scotland@fostering.net*
*www.fostering.net/scotland/*

# Other organisations

## Infertility Network UK

Infertility Network UK is the national self-help organisation which provides information, support and representation to people with fertility difficulties and those who work with them.

**Infertility Network UK**
Charter House
43 St Leonards Road
Bexhill on Sea
East Sussex TN40 1JA
*Tel: 0800 008 7464*
*Email: admin@infertilitynetworkuk.com*
*www.infertilitynetworkuk.com*

## Intercountry Adoption Centre

The Intercountry Adoption Centre offers advice and information about current policy and practice in relation to overseas adoption and the legal requirements of the UK and "sending" countries. It produces a useful information pack with information about particular countries, and also runs group events.

**Intercountry Adoption Centre**
22 Union Street
Barnet
Hertfordshire
EN5 4HZ
*Tel: 020 8447 4753/ 020 8449 2562*

*Email: info@icacentre.org.uk*
*www.icacentre.org.uk*

## Independent Review Mechanism England and Independent Review Mechanism Cymru

### Independent Review Mechanism (IRM) England
Unit 4 Pavilion Business Park
Royds Hall Road
Wortley
Leeds
LS12 6AJ
*Tel: 0845 450 3956*
*Email: irm@baaf.org.uk*
*www.independentreviewmechanism.org.uk*

### Independent Review Mechanism Cymru
7 Cleeve House
Lambourne Crescent
Cardiff
CF14 5GP
*Tel: 0845 873 1305*
*Email: irm@irmcymru.org.uk*
*www.irmcymru.org.uk*

# Useful reading

Except where marked, these publications are available from BAAF.
Visit www.baaf.org.uk or contact BAAF Publications on 020 7421
2604 for more details or to order.

## Books about adoption

### PERSONAL NARRATIVES BY ADOPTERS

#### An Adoption Diary

MARIA JAMES

This is an inspirational real-life account of one couple's emotional
journey to become a family, which gives a fascinating insight into
adoption today. Spanning four years, the diary covers assessment,
the months of waiting, and finally the match with a two-year-old
boy.

*BAAF 2006*

#### Flying Solo

JULIA WISE

Julia Wise gave up a high-flying career and hectic London life to
move to the country and adopt a child on her own. This heartwarming and humorous account will resonate loudly with single
adopters everywhere.

*BAAF 2007*

#### In Black and White

NATHALIE SEYMOUR

This honest account follows Nathalie and Tom, a white couple living
in 1970s Britain, who decided to establish a transracial adopted
family. Further, they wanted the children to remain connected with
their birth family. An intriguing and absorbing story.

*BAAF 2007*

## Adoption Undone
KAREN CARR

This is the true story of an adoption and an adoption breakdown, bravely told by the adoptive mother. From the final court hearing when Lucy returned to local authority care, Karen Carr looks back over a tale of loss and regret, but also courage, generosity and self-discovery.

*BAAF 2007*

## Together in Time
RUTH AND ED ROYCE

From a dual perspective, each with their own anxieties and expectations, Ruth and Ed Royce record their decision to adopt, their son's deep-seated problems, and how their experience of music and art therapy helped them to come together as a family...and to adopt for a second time.

*BAAF 2008*

## The Family Business
ROBERT MARSDEN

This is the story of the adoption of William, a little boy with cerebral palsy, by a middle-aged couple with three birth children. Narrated by the adoptive father, this positive, upbeat account describes adopting a child with a disability and the impact of adoption on the whole family.

*BAAF 2008*

## Take Two
LAUREL ASHTON

This moving story follows Laurel and David through their discovery of their infertility, months of treatment, and eventual decision to adopt. Their adoption of Amber, a baby girl, and then of Emily, are narrated, as Laurel remembers the first months of family life.

*BAAF 2008*

### Dale's Tale

HELEN JAYNE

The story of Helen, a foster carer, and her family, and what happened when a short-term foster placement – of Dale, a young boy – became longer than expected. When Helen decides she wants to adopt Dale, the agencies involved have other ideas.

*BAAF 2010*

### Holding on and Hanging in

JACKIE WHITE

This compelling journey tracks Wayne's journey, from first being fostered by Lorna at the age of nine, in a "therapeutic" foster placement, through nearly four years of family life. Wayne is traumatised by his early experiences, and helping him to heal and grow is a long and difficult process, but Lorna is determined to persevere.

*BAAF 2010*

### Frozen

MIKE BUTCHER

When husband and wife Mike and Lesley embark on a course of IVF treatment, they are full of hope for a successful outcome – a child they can call their own. But after a shocking reaction to the treatment, and an escalating series of setbacks and heartache, they are forced to put their dream on hold – until they look into adoption.

*BAAF 2010*

### When Daisy met Tommy

JULES BELLE

This is the real-life story of how six-year-old Daisy and her parents adopted Tom. Honest and accessible, it charts the ups and downs of the adoption process, as experienced by a daughter already in the family.

*BAAF 2010*

## Becoming Dads

PABLO FERNÁNDEZ

This is the story of Pablo and Mike, and their journey to adoption. Set against a backdrop of diverse perceptions as to whether gay men should adopt, Pablo's narrative tracks them through approaching an agency, being approved, and finally adopting a young boy.

***BAAF 2011***

## Is it True you have Two Mums?

RUBY CLAY

The heartwarming story of Ruby and Gail, who adopt three daughters, through different routes, as a lesbian dual-heritage couple.

***BAAF 2011***

## Finding our Familia

STEVAN WHITEHEAD

Stevan Whitehead tells the story of his family's adoption of two children from Guatemala, but also their many subsequent trips to the country, their supportive links with their new-found extended family, and the way they help their children maintain links with their origins.

***BAAF 2012***

## ADOPTION: DIFFERENT ASPECTS

### The Adopter's Handbook

AMY NEIL SALTER

This guide sets out clear, accurate information about adoption before, during and after the big event, to help adopters help themselves throughout the adoption process and beyond. Topics covered include education, health and adoption support.

***BAAF 2013 (4th edition)***

## Attachment, Trauma and Resilience
KATE CAIRNS
Drawing on Kate's personal experiences with three birth children and 12 fostered children, this book describes family life with children who have experienced attachment difficulties, loss and trauma. Using knowledge and ideas drawn from attachment theory, the author suggests what can be done to promote recovery and develop resilience.
*BAAF 2002*

## Adopters on Adoption: Reflections on parenthood and children
DAVID HOWE
In this absorbing collection of personal stories, adoptive parents whose children are now young adults describe the importance and distinctiveness of adoptive parenting.
*BAAF 1996*

## Related by Adoption: A handbook for grandparents and other carers
HEDI ARGENT
This handbook aims to give grandparents and other relatives information about adoption today that directly affects them. It discusses how the wider family can support building a family through adoption and be involved in both the good and the bad times.
*BAAF 2012*

## Could you be my Parent?
EDITED BY LEONIE STURGE-MOORE
This enthralling anthology gathers together a selection of informative, often moving articles and interviews from Be My Parent, BAAF's family-finding newspaper, to create a fascinating snapshot of the process of adoption and foster care.
*BAAF 2005*

### 'Just a member of the family': Families and children who adopt
BRIDGET BETTS, VIDEO/DVD
This is the first film to look at adoption from a child's point of view, featuring a number of birth children who have had the experience of adopting a child into their family.
*BAAF 2005*

### Chosen: Writing and poetry by adopted children and young people
EDITED BY PERLITA HARRIS
Intensely moving, this collection of prose, poetry and artwork from 80 adopted children and young people, aged from 4 to 20 years of age, reveals how it feels and what it means to be adopted.
*BAAF 2008*

### The Adoption Experience: Families who give children a second chance
ANN MORRIS
Actual adopters tell it like it is on every part of the adoption process from the exciting moment of first deciding to adopt to feelings about children seeking a reunion with their natural families or simply leaving home.
*Jessica Kingsley Publishers for Adoption UK 1999*

## ADOPTION: PARENTING

### Why was I Adopted?
JANE JACKSON
A short guide which looks at some of the most common big adoption questions that adopted children ask, and explores the feelings and worries that can lie behind the questions, with suggested dialogues.
*BAAF 2013*

## Talking about Adoption to your Adopted Child
MARJORIE MORRISON

A guide to the whys, whens, and hows of telling adopted children about their origins at different ages and stages and including a range of subjects.

***BAAF 2012***

## Adoption Conversations: What, when and how to tell
RENÉE WOLFS

This in-depth practical guide, written by an adoptive parent, explores the questions adopted children are likely to ask, with suggestions for helpful answers. Although the guide focuses primarily on children adopted from abroad, the advice is applicable to any adopted child. A second book, *More Adoption Conversations* (2010), by the same author, looks at adopted young people aged 13–18.

***BAAF 2008***

## Looking After our Own: The stories of black and Asian adopters
EDITED BY HOPE MASSIAH

An inspiring collection looking at the experiences of nine black and Asian adoptive families and their children.

***BAAF 2005***

## Whatever Happened to Adam? Stories about disabled children who were adopted or fostered
HEDI ARGENT

This remarkable book tells the stories of 20 young people with disabilities and the families who chose to care for them. Following their life journeys from joining their new families, through childhood and adolescence, it reveals the tremendous rewards of adopting or fostering a disabled child.

***BAAF 1998***

## First Steps in Parenting the Child who Hurts: Tiddlers and toddlers
CAROLINE ARCHER

This book offers practical, sensitive guidance from an adoptive parent through the areas of separation, loss and trauma in early childhood which will encourage confidence in other adoptive parents and foster carers and thereby enable enjoyment in parenting young children.

*Jessica Kingsley Publishers for Adoption UK 1999 (2nd edition)*

## Next Steps in Parenting the Child who Hurts: Tykes and teens
CAROLINE ARCHER

Follows on from the First Steps book and shows how love can be expressed towards the older adopted child, despite persistent and often extreme tests of that love. Includes a review of specific sensitive situations that commonly arise and suggests some solutions.

*Jessica Kingsley Publishers for Adoption UK 1999*

## Form ICA
Intercountry adoption form (medical report and development assessment of child) which, when ordered individually, comes with two copies of Form AH for the prospective adoptive parents.

# Advice Notes

BAAF's popular leaflet series called Advice Notes contains essential information about key areas in adoption and fostering.

## Adoption – some questions answered (2010)
Basic information about adoption. Explains the adoption process including the legal issues and the rights of birth parents.

## Foster care – some questions answered (2010)
Basic information about fostering. Explains different types of foster care and the relationship with the local authority.

### The preparation and assessment process (adoption) (2010)
Aimed at prospective adopters who have started the process with an agency. Explores preparation and assessment and what it involves.

### The preparation and assessment process (fostering) (2010)
Aimed at prospective foster carers who have started the process with an agency. Explores preparation and assessment and what it involves.

### Children's special needs – some questions answered (2012)
Information on the special needs that adopted and fostered children may have, for people considering adopting or fostering.

### Private fostering (2009)
Aimed at those considering private fostering in England and Wales, this leaflet explains what private fostering involves, and what prospective carers need to know.

### Special guardianship (2010)
Provides information about the difference between special guardianship and other forms of permanence for children.

### Stepchildren and adoption (2012)
Information for birth parents and step-parents on the advantages or not of adoption, and obtaining further advice. Editions available for England and Wales or Scotland.

### Intercountry adoption – information and guidance (2011)
Information on adopting a child from overseas, including procedures, legislation, and where to obtain advice.

### Children adopted from abroad – key health and developmental issues (2004)
Gives advice on the health and medical issues you may encounter if adopting a child from overseas.

# Periodicals listing children who need new families

### Be My Parent and Be My Parent online
A UK-wide monthly newspaper and website for adopters and permanent foster carers who may or may not be approved. It contains features on adoption and fostering and profiles of children across the UK who need new permanent families. Subscription details available from: 020 7421 2666.

### Scottish Children Waiting
Scotland's Adoption Register produces a newsletter of children awaiting placement in Scotland. This is distributed to local authorities and voluntary adoption agencies and is available to approved adopters and long-term foster carers.
*Tel: 0131 226 9279*

### Adoption Today
Adoption Today is a monthly magazine published by Adoption UK and is available on subscription. It keeps members in touch with one another, profiles children needing new permanent families, and gives information on general developments in the field of adoption. Adoption UK also provides the family-finding newspaper and website *Children who Wait*.
*Adoption UK Tel: 01295 752240*


BAAF produces a large variety of other books about adoption, including a wide selection of books for use with children. For more details, visit www.baaf.org.uk or contact 020 7421 2604 for a catalogue.

# Glossary

Below is a glossary of certain terms that appear in the book. In cases where there is a difference between England and Wales and Scotland, this is shown.

## Accommodated/Accommodation

### England and Wales

Under section 20 of the Children Act 1989, the local authority is required to "provide accommodation" for children "in need" in certain circumstances. The local authority does not acquire parental responsibility (see below) merely by accommodating a child and the arrangements for the child must normally be agreed with the parent(s), who, subject to certain circumstances, are entitled to remove the children from local authority accommodation at any time. They retain parental responsibility. A child who is accommodated is a 'looked after child' (see below).

### Scotland

Under section 25 of the Children (Scotland) Act 1995, the local authority must "provide accommodation" for children in certain circumstances and may also do so in other situations. Normally, the accommodation is provided by agreement with the parent(s), they can then remove the child at any time in most circumstances. Parental responsibilities remain with the parent(s). A child accommodated under section 25 is a "looked after child" (see below).

## Adoption panel

Adoption agencies (local authorities or voluntary adoption societies) are required to set up an adoption panel which must consider and make recommendations on children for whom adoption is the plan, on prospective adopters and on matches between prospective adopters and children.

# Adoption placement plan

A term used in England. A plan that gives information to the prospective adopter about the child when the agency has decided to place the child with them. It sets out, for example, when the child will move into the prospective adopter's home, parental responsibility, adoption support services, contact with the child, and arrangements for reviewing the placement.

# Adoption placement report

A term used in England. A report prepared by the adoption agency for the adoption panel which sets out, for example, the reasons for proposing the placement, arrangements for allowing any person contact with the child, the prospective adopter's view on the proposed placement, and, where the agency is a local authority, proposals for providing adoption support services for the adoptive family.

# Adoption Register for England and Wales

A database of approved prospective adopters and children waiting for adoption across England and Wales. A team of experienced social workers will use the database to link children with approved prospective adopters where local matches cannot be found.

# Adoption Register – Scotland

Scotland's Adoption Register operates in a similar way to the Adoption Register for England and Wales, for approved adopters and children living in Scotland.

# Adoption Regional Information System (ARIS)

A scheme similar to the Adoption Register, for approved adopters and children living in Northern Ireland.

## Adoption Support Agency (ASA)

An organisation or person registered, under Part 2 of the Care Standards Act 2000, to provide adoption support services. An ASA may operate on a profit or not-for-profit basis.

## Adult Attachment Interview (AAI)

A tool for assessing an adult's attachment style, based on asking about the adult's experience of being parented. It is used by trained assessors, largely as a research tool.

## Annex A report

A court report in relation to an adoption application in England.

## Article 15 report

A report prepared on the prospective adopter under Article 15 of the Convention on Protection of Children and Co-operation in respect of Intercountry Adoption (the Hague Convention). This includes information on their identity, eligibility and suitability to adopt, background, family and medical history, social environment, reasons for adoption, ability to undertake an intercountry adoption and the characteristics of the children for whom they would be qualified to care.

## Article 16 information

A report prepared on the child under Article 16 of the Hague Convention. This includes information on his/her identity, adoptability, background, social environment, family history, medical history including that of the child's family, and any special needs of the child.

## Attachment Style Interview (ASI)

An assessment tool used to assess the characteristics of carers in terms of their quality of close relationships, social support and security of attachment style. It is used by trained assessors.

## CAFCASS

The Children and Family Court Advisory and Support Service is a national non-departmental public body for England. It has brought together the services provided by the Family Court Welfare Service, the Guardian ad Litem Services and the Children's Division of the Official Solicitor. CAFCASS is independent of the courts, social services, education and health authorities and all similar agencies. A CAFCASS officer must formally witness the consent to adoption of a birth parent.

## CAMHS (Child and Adolescent Mental Health Services)

Services that contribute to the mental health care of children and young people, whether provided by health, education or social services or other agencies. CAMHS cover all types of provision and intervention, including individual therapy for children, mental health promotion and primary prevention and specialist community-based services.

## Care Order

Applies only to England and Wales. A child who is subject to a Care Order is described as being "in care". A Care Order is a court order which gives the local authority parental responsibility for the child but does not deprive the parent(s) of this. Nevertheless, the local authority may limit the extent to which parents may exercise their parental responsibility and may override parental wishes in the interests of the child's welfare.

## Care plan

An agreed plan for looking after a child and meeting the child's
current and future needs, made by the placing authority under the
Children Act 1989. The care plan will be presented to court when a
care order is applied for.

## Child's Permanence Report (CPR)

A report required under English regulations when adoption is the
plan for a child. It should include comprehensive information on the
child, their birth family, the reasons for the adoption plan, proposed
contact arrangements, and the views of the birth parents and child
on the plan.

## Children's guardian

Applies only to England and Wales. A person working for CAFCASS
and appointed by the court to safeguard a child's interests in court
proceedings (formerly called a guardian ad litem). Their duties are set
out in court rules and include presenting a report to the court.

## Concurrent planning

A scheme in which children, usually babies or toddlers, for whom
there is a chance that they might return home to their birth family,
are placed with families who will foster them with this aim. However,
the foster carers are also approved as adopters and will adopt the
child should the planned return to the birth family not be successful.
In this way, the moves that a child may otherwise have to make are
minimised. These schemes have to be run with the agreement and
co-operation of the local courts and to tight timescales.

# Consortium

A group of usually not more than six–eight local adoption agencies, often both local authorities and voluntary adoption agencies, who share details of waiting families and children in order to try and make speedy local placements for children.

# Contact/Contact Order

**England and Wales**
Contact may be used to mean visits, including residential visits or other form of direct face-to-face contact between a child and another individual, or it may mean indirect ways of keeping in touch, e.g. letters or telephone calls including letters sent via a third party. Once a local authority is authorised to place a child for adoption, there is no presumption for or against contact. The child's needs will be the paramount consideration.

**Scotland**
As in England and Wales, contact can mean direct or indirect contact or access. It covers private arrangements (e.g. in divorce, etc); it also covers a public law situation when a child is "looked after" by a local authority. When a child is on a supervision requirement (see below) under the Children's Hearing system, the hearing regulates contact.

# Couple

Two people (whether of different sexes or the same sex) living as partners (married or unmarried) in an enduring family relationship. This does not include two people one of whom is the other's parent, grandparent, sister, brother, aunt or uncle.

# Curator ad litem

Similar to children's guardian in England and Wales (see above).

## Decision-maker

A senior person within the agency who is a social worker with at least three years' post-qualifying experience in child care social work. The decision-maker makes the final decision, after considering the recommendation of the adoption panel and, in some cases, of the independent review panel. There may be more than one decision-maker but all must be qualified as above.

## Disclosure and Barring Service (DBS)

An agency which provides access to criminal records and other information. In relation to adoption and fostering, the DBS provides enhanced disclosures on prospective adopters and foster carers and members of their households to the adoption or fostering agency.

## Disruption

The unplanned ending of an adoption or permanent fostering placement, usually, in the case of adoption, before the Adoption Order is made. A disruption meeting will usually be arranged so that as much as possible can be learnt from the experience to inform future practice.

## Fast-track approval process

This is available to anyone who is an approved foster carer in England and to people who have previously adopted in a court in England or Wales under the Adoption Agencies Regulations 2005 (or Welsh equivalent). It enables these individuals to enter the adoption approval process at Stage Two. Agencies are required to complete the process within four months.

# Fostering/foster care

In this book this term is used for those cases where a child is placed with a foster carer approved by the local authority and/or placed directly by a voluntary organisation. These placements are governed by the Fostering Services Regulations 2002 in England and by the Looked After Children (Scotland) Regulations 2009. "Short-term", "long-term" and "permanent" foster care and "respite care" may mean different things to different people – they are not legally defined terms.

# Fostering for Adoption (FFA)

Under Fostering for Adoption, an agency can give an approved adopter temporary approval as a foster carer for a named child. This enables a child to be placed as a foster child with carers without them having had a full fostering assessment or panel approval as foster carers. These will be children for whom the likelihood of eventual adoption is high. However, the child is fostered until, in most cases, work with birth parents and court involvement enables an adoption plan to be agreed and the child to be matched for adoption with these carers at panel.

# Freeing Order/freeing for adoption

### England and Wales

A Freeing Order under the Adoption Act 1976 ends parents' parental responsibility and transfers parental responsibility to the adoption agency. The purpose of this is to allow any issue regarding parental consent to adoption to be resolved before the child is placed with prospective adopters. In certain circumstances the "former parent" may ask the court to revoke the order if the child is not placed with prospective adopters after one year. Freeing orders can no longer be applied for (from 30 December 2005) but existing freeing orders remain in force and authorise the local authority to place a child for adoption.

## Guardian

A guardian is a person who has been formally appointed as a child's guardian after the death of one or both parents. The appointment may be made in writing by a parent or by a court.

## Independent Review Mechanism (IRM) England

This is only available to people assessed by an adoption agency in England, and is a review process that is conducted by an independent review panel. The prospective adopter may initiate this process when their adoption agency has made a qualifying determination. The review panel reviews the case and gives a fresh recommendation to the agency.

## Independent Review Mechanism (IRM) Cymru

This is only available to people assessed by an adoption agency in Wales. It operates in the same way as the IRM, described above.

## Independent Reviewing Officer (IRO)

Chairs statutory child care reviews for looked after children. He or she is independent of the child's social work team and of budget holders.

## Interagency placement

A child looked after by one local authority may be placed with adopters approved by another adoption agency. An interagency fee is usually paid by the child's agency to the family's agency to reimburse that agency for their work.

# Kinship care

Sometimes called family and friends care. This is when a child is looked after by a relative or someone already well known to them.

# Later life letter

A letter written by the child's social worker to the child summarising some of the life story information. For young children, it is information which their adoptive parents will share with them in due course.

# Life story work/book

This is work which should be done with the child by their social worker, in co-operation with their foster carers and their birth family if possible. Its aim is to give the child as clear a picture as possible of what has happened in their life and why they are now being placed for adoption. It is an opportunity for the child to express their feelings about what has happened so far. A life story book should be completed with the child, with photos, drawings and an age-appropriate account of their life so far. The process of assimilating this information and making sense of it may well take many years and the child will need ongoing help and support from his or her adoptive parents.

# Looked after

### England and Wales
This term includes both children "in care" and accommodated children. Local authorities have certain duties towards all looked after children and their parents, which are set out in Part III of the Children Act 1989. These include the duty to safeguard and promote the child's welfare and the duty to consult with children and parents before taking decisions.

**Scotland**

This term covers all children for whom the local authority has responsibilities under section 17 of the Children (Scotland) Act 1995. It replaces the term "in care". It is wider than and different from the English and Welsh definition. It includes children who remain at home as well as those placed away from home.

## Non-agency adoption

An adoption where the child has not been placed by an adoption agency. The majority of these are adoptions by step-parents.

## Open adoption

This term may be used very loosely and can mean anything from an adoption where a child continues to have frequent face-to-face contact with members of his or her birth family to an adoption where there is some degree of "openness", e.g. the birth family and adopters meeting each other once. People using the term should be asked to define what they mean!

## Parental responsibility

**England and Wales**

This is defined in the Children Act 1989 as 'all the rights, duties, powers and responsibilities which by law a parent has in relation to a child and his property'. When a child is born to married parents, they will both share parental responsibility for him or her, and this parental responsibility can never be lost except on the making of an Adoption Order. A father who is not married to the child's mother does not automatically have parental responsibility but may acquire it either by being named on the birth certificate (from December 2003), by formal agreement with the mother or by court order. Adoptive parents in England and Wales acquire parental responsibility when a child is placed with them, although the local authority placing the child can restrict their exercise of this until the Adoption Order is made.

### Parental responsibilities and rights – Scotland

These are what parents have for their children and are defined in sections 1 and 2 of the Children (Scotland) Act 1995. All mothers acquire them automatically when children are born. Fathers acquire them automatically at birth if they are married to the mother at conception or later. Fathers also acquire them automatically at birth if they are shown on the birth certificates for any children registered on or after 4 May 2006. Fathers can also get them by formal agreement with the mother, or by court order.

Anyone can go to court for an order about parental responsibilities and rights under section 11 of the Children (Scotland) Act 1995. Residence Orders (see below) and Contact Orders (see above) are examples. The court can also take away responsibilities and rights under this section.

Parents or others with responsibilities and rights can only lose them by a court order: an Adoption Order; or a Permanence Order (see below).

In relation to a father who is not married to the mother, the father can obtain these rights through an agreement under the Children (Scotland) Act 1995.

## Permanence Order

This is an order used in Scotland under the Adoption and Children (Scotland) Act 2007. It is for children who cannot live with their birth families. It gives some parental responsibilities and rights to the local authority, gives other parental responsibilities and rights to appropriate people, including foster carers, and leaves some responsibilities and rights with the child's parents, if that is in the child's best interests. This order provides flexibility to adapt to a child's changing circumstances. It can remove parental rights and responsibilities and give authority for placement for adoption.

## Permanent fostering

The aim of permanent fostering is to provide a child with a secure base in a family until they are adult and beyond. However, it lacks the greater legal security of special guardianship or, especially, of adoption.

## Placement Order

An order made by the court under section 21 of the Adoption and Children Act 2002 authorising a local authority to place a child for adoption with any prospective adopters who may be chosen by the authority. It continues in force until it is revoked, or an Adoption Order is made in respect of the child, or the child marries, forms a civil partnership or attains the age of 18. Only local authorities may apply for Placement Orders.

## Prospective adopter's report (PAR)

A report prepared by an adoption agency when the approval of a prospective adopter is being considered.

- *Full report* – includes, for example, the prospective adopter's date of birth, identifying information, ethnic origin, cultural/linguistic background, religious persuasion, description of his/her personality, whether he/she is single or a member of a couple, the agency' assessment of his/her suitability to adopt a child, and a summary of his/her state of health.
- *Brief report* – the agency does not need to complete a full report where it receives information that leads it to consider that the prospective adopter may not be suitable to adopt a child. That information would be either that set out in Part 1, Schedule 4 of the Adoption Agencies Regulations 2005, or the health report, or the report of interviews with referees, or the local authority report, or other information.

# Qualifying determination

A term used in England and Wales. In relation to suitability to adopt a child – a determination is made by an adoption agency that it considers a prospective adopter is not suitable to be an adoptive parent and does not propose to approve him/her as suitable to be an adoptive parent.

# Reporting officer

A member of the panel of curators ad litem and reporting officers, appointed by the court for adoption proceedings. His or her specific task is to ensure that the agreement of a parent or guardian to an Adoption Order, if given, is given freely and with full understanding of what is involved and to witness the agreement.

# Residence Order

**England and Wales**
An order under the Children Act 1989 settling the arrangements as to the person/s with whom the child is to live. Where a Residence Order is made in favour of someone who does not already have parental responsibility for the child (e.g. a relative or foster carer), that person will acquire parental responsibilities subject to certain restrictions (e.g. they will not be able to consent to the child's adoption). Parental responsibility given in connection with a Residence Order will only last as long as the Residence Order. A Residence Order normally only lasts until the child's 16th birthday.

**Scotland**
This is one of the orders possible under section 11 of the Children (Scotland) Act 1995. It regulates with whom the child lives. If the person with the Residence Order did not have any parental responsibilities and rights before, the order gives those as well.

# Residence Order allowance

### England and Wales
Local authorities have a power to contribute to the cost of a child's maintenance when the child is living with somebody under a Residence Order provided he or she is not living with a parent or step-parent. A financial contribution under this power is normally referred to as a Residence Order allowance.

### Scotland
Local authorities have the power to pay an allowance to a person who has care of a child and who is not a parent or a foster carer. The person does not have to have a Residence Order.

# Special Guardianship Order

An order in England and Wales under the Adoption and Children Act 2002 offering an alternative legal status for children. The child is no longer looked after. It gives the special guardian parental responsibility which he or she can exercise to the exclusion of others. However, the birth parent(s) retain parental responsibility. Support services, including financial support, are very similar to those for adopters.

# Stage One – pre-assessment process (England)

This stage of the adoption process in England starts once an agency has accepted a Registration of Interest from an individual. It should normally be completed within two months. Should it take longer, it must be recorded on the prospective adopter's case record. A Stage One plan should be agreed with the prospective adopter. Initial training and preparation will be given, and all prescribed checks and references will be carried out. Where an agency decides that a prospective adopter is not suitable to adopt during or at the end of this stage, it must inform the individual in writing with a clear explanation of the reasons. Prospective adopters may make a complaint, but have no recourse to the Independent Review Mechanism (IRM).

## Stage Two – the assessment process (England)

Prospective adopters in England are not able to start this part of the process until they have successfully completed Stage One. Stage Two should take four months to the final decision, unless there are exceptional circumstances or the prospective adopter asks for a delay. Reasons should be recorded on the case file. A written Assessment Plan should be prepared with the prospective adopter. This stage covers an assessment of the prospective adopter's suitability to adopt and should include any necessary intensive training. A prospective adopter's report (PAR) is completed, an adoption panel considers the case, and a decision-maker makes a final decision.

## Supervision requirements

Applies only to Scotland. These are the orders made by the Children's Hearing for any child needing compulsory measures of supervision. Children may be victims of abuse or neglect, have other problems and/or have committed crimes. All children on supervision requirements are "looked after" by the local authority, even if they live at home. Supervision requirements do not give parental responsibilities and rights to local authorities.

## Twin-track, parallel or contingency planning

These are all names given to planning for a looked after child for adoption or long-term fostering while at the same time considering the possibility of placement with birth parents or with extended family members.

# Read about adoption

**Adoption Undone**

*Flying Solo*
Julia Wise

*An Adoption Diary*
A couple's journey into parenthood
Maria James

*Take t...*
Laurel Ashton

## Stories by adopters
Poignant insights into the highs and lows of adoption revealed through the real life experiences of a wide range of families.

## Guides for adopters
Practical and accessible handbooks, packed with a wealth of information and advice, on caring for and communicating with adopted children.

A handbook for grandparents and other relatives

*Related by Adoption*
Hedi Argent

THE **PINK GUIDE** TO **ADOPTION** FOR LESBIANS AND GAY MEN

The **PRIMAL WOUND**
Understanding the adopted child

*Adoption conversations*
What, when and how to tell

*Special & odd*
A fascinating a...
womxnly t...
Jenny Mal...

**Mother M...**
"A brave and compelling book"

*The Colours in me*
An a...
w...
jou...
moth...
Edited by...
Zara H Phillips

## Reflections by adoptees
Adopted children and adults explore, in their own words, what it feels like and what it means to be adopted.

**And much more...**
## visit www.baaf.org.uk

BAAF
ADOPTION & FOSTERING

British Association for Adoption & Fostering (BAAF), Saffron House, 6-10 Kirby Street, London EC1N 8TS.
Charity registration 275689 (England and Wales) and SC039337 (Scotland)